Justice and Equality

Here and Now

Justice and Equality Here and Now

Edited by FRANK S. LUCASH

Contributions by

JUDITH N. SHKLAR, CHARLES TAYLOR,
ALLAN BLOOM, WILLIAM GALSTON,
G. A. COHEN, MICHAEL WALZER,
AND WALTER BERNS

Cornell University Press

ITHACA AND LONDON

First published 1986 by Cornell University Press.

International Standard Book Number (cloth) 0–8014–1807–0
International Standard Book Number (paper) 0–8014–9350–1
Library of Congress Catalog Card Number 85–19465
Printed in the United States of America
Librarians: Library of Congress cataloging information
appears on the last page of the book.

The paper in this book is acid-free and meets the guidelines for
permanence and durability of the Committee on Production Guidelines
for Book Longevity of the Council on Library Resources.

Contents

Preface

This highly diverse collection of essays by a group of prominent philosophers and political theorists makes a comprehensive contribution to the vigorous ongoing debate on justice and equality. The publication of John Rawls's *Theory of Justice* (1971) and Robert Nozick's *Anarchy, State, and Utopia* (1974) challenged scholars to speculate afresh on the foundations of distributive justice and its relationship to other kinds of human good. From the outset, their arguments have had direct implications for the quotidian clashes of those who decide the distribution of goods and opportunities in our democratic society. This blurring of the traditional line between philosophy and partisan politics has enriched the scholarly discussion and opened it up to an unprecedentedly wide audience. The present volume, which collects new work by seven thinkers who have made notable — and often conflicting — contributions to this debate, should therefore attract all those who care deeply about the future of justice in democratic societies.

An introductory essay that surveys the problems explored by the other contributors to this volume is followed by a paper that discusses the history of the philosophical tradition of equality and justice. The three succeeding papers present varying perspectives on the philosophical foundations of modern egalitarianism and inegalitarianism. The two final essays offer opposing views on the current debate on equality.

In her introductory essay, Judith Shklar responds to some leading theories about justice and equality by offering a defense of individual rights, seen through the eyes of the American Scholar, who has visions of a common political order. This scholar is influenced by Locke's state of nature and natural rights and Aristotle's social ethos and doctrine of equilibrium. Shklar believes that rights need to be understood as protests and refusals in response to failures of justice. Rights are not only demands for more shares but expressions of fear of being injured or treated with cruelty by more powerful forces.

Charles Taylor raises questions about the nature of distributive justice and its relation to different notions of the human good. In order to answer these questions properly, he argues, we must deal with our social nature (an Aristotelian view) rather than with human rights (a Lockean view). Two kinds of arguments arise in the social perspective: one about the framework for the principles of distributive justice, the other about the principles themselves. In the second part of his paper, he examines these principles by discussing equality and inequality in societies today. What he recommends is a certain degree of equality and a more equal balance of mutual indebtedness.

Allan Bloom tells us that, according to Rousseau, men and women have different functions, naturally and socially. Women bear and nurse children and have an instinctive attachment to them. Society is constructed out of this bond between mother and child. Rousseau believes in the natural goodness of human sexual desire. This desire, elevated to love by way of the family, ennobles human beings and strengthens the political order. Modesty enables women to have power over men. Women need this power to start the family and hold it together. Women are free to choose their husbands, and any legal obligations must be supported by natural inclinations. Freedom is obedience to the law one lays down for oneself. The social contract originates in the sexual contract.

William Galston attempts to provide a foundation for warding off attacks against equality of opportunity. He holds that justice is relative to the individual and depends on a view of the good life. In discussing the good life, he proposes a notion of human equality that is essential to equality of opportunity: the full development of any one individual is equal in moral weight to that of any other individual. This concept, along with the notion of individual desert, is a requirement of a just society.

G. A. Cohen attacks Robert Nozick's view that inequality of private property and inequality of condition stem from each person's morally rightful ownership of him- or herself. He believes that by holding on to self-ownership one does not bring about the inegalitarian distribution of worldly resources that Nozick claims one does. In opposition to the usual left response, Cohen suggests an affirmation or at least a nondenial of the thesis of self-ownership, along with an egalitarian approach to external goods. The second part of his paper is concerned with the question of how private property was originally appropriated.

Michael Walzer discusses the way in which human beings can live together in our society without oppressing and injuring one another. In order to do so, he believes, we must have a shared economic, social, and cultural infrastructure; the construction and maintenance of such things as highways, parks, and museums must be decided democratically, not by private groups. Second, the first commitment of the state must be to take care of its weakest members. Third, equality of opportunity is possible only when limits are imposed on the exercise of office, wealth, and power, and when the range of opportunities is broadened. Fourth, political power must be widely available to citizens, and alternatives to the corporate power structure should be explored.

Walter Berns points out that according to the framers of the Constitution, all men are equally endowed with the rights to life, liberty, and the pursuit of happiness and that a state should be built in order to secure these rights. Although individuals are equal in the possession of these rights, they are not equal in the faculty of acquiring property. Some people are more enterprising than others. Society profits from the enterprising person, although the rights of others are still protected.

I am grateful to the Paul A. Leonard family of Reno for their generous support of a conference held from September 22 to 24, 1983, in Reno at which six of the seven papers in this book were presented, and to the UNR Foundation, the Nevada Humanities Committee, and the National Endowment for the Humanities. I was assisted in adding an introductory essay by the Graduate School of the University of Nevada at Reno. The conference could not have been organized without the help of my colleagues John Kelly, Deborah Achtenberg, Piotr Hoffman, and Thomas Nickles, and of our secretary, Elisa Lazzari. John Ackerman of Cornell University Press has been helpful in bringing this book to publication.

Frank S. Lucash

Reno, Nevada

Justice and Equality

Here and Now

[1]

Injustice, Injury, and Inequality: An Introduction

JUDITH N. SHKLAR

The publication of John Rawls's *Theory of Justice* was a great event not only because of its intrinsic excellence but also because it freed many of its readers from a long, self-imposed philosophical silence.[1] Anglo-American philosophers had taken a vow to say nothing substantive about morality or politics. They were determined not to compromise the rational purposes of conceptual clarification with expressions of purely personal feeling. The impartiality and impersonality of reason were their first obligation and they were not eager to become preachers or propagandists. The ideological excesses of the time and their results surely contributed much initially to this affirmation of uncontaminated styles of thought. It was an altogether honorable and responsible reaction, but it had its frustrations, especially as the political and moral horrors amid which we live did not abate. The instant achievement of *A Theory of Justice* was to show that questions of great ethical urgency, such as the proper balance between liberty and equality, could be discussed without the slightest loss of rational rigor or philosophical rectitude. Arguments for and against every proposition could be weighed and a conclusion drawn without a trace of dogmatism or self-indul-

1. John Rawls, *A Theory of Justice* (Cambridge: Belknap Press of Harvard University Press, 1971).

gence. This realization was nothing less than a revelation to the book's first readers, and its inspiring effect will surely be enduring. Both philosophers and social theorists found direction in its pages. For the former the structure of the book's arguments and the force of its examples and counterexamples gave a new life to the old conflict between Kant and the utilitarians. For the latter it provided a new way of thinking about historical institutions and political practices. The intellectual consequences of Rawls's book will surely be more enduring than the ideological outbursts that it has provoked. Philosophers are not likely to return to their antiseptic bubble, even if much of their work will remain too abstract to have much bearing on historical or psychological experiences. One must also expect that a lot of tiresome ideological infighting will continue. Nevertheless, Rawls's work is remarkable enough to justify all its own consequences, even the appearance of a small army of squabbling heirs.

How can, how do we talk about redistributing resources more justly now? Trend watching is not a rewarding exercise at any time, and when as many voices speak simultaneously as we find in this volume and in so many similar ones, it is altogether futile. Nevertheless, it is worthwhile at least to note the intellectual boundaries, however flexible they may be, within which theories about justice and equality move back and forth. One can try to arrest the passing moment long enough to recognize a few leading theories and to respond to them. Some recurrent phrases, concerns, and tensions can be readily discerned and noted to that end.

Amid the multitude of theoretical suggestions some stand out as novel or insistent or both. Not policies alone but the way we are to think about persons and their ethical structure are in dispute. Thus our "intuitions" about what is good and evil, right and wrong, are now to be taken more seriously than they once were. What, however, is an intuition? Whose intuitions count and whose do not? What is their worth and how vague are they? When a statement is said to be counterintuitive, one is asking for additional arguments, because one still feels uneasy. Such an assertion is not at all like a flat statement about "our intuitions" which is to be taken as a firm starting point for, or even an end to, an argument. Behind those self-evident intuitions there stands a rather uncontested moral realism that takes "our" morality as given. It halts disputes rather than encouraging and renewing them. Thus "community" has joined "citizenship" as a tremendously "plus" word in "our" vocabulary. Without it no social reform, perhaps no ethical life at all, is thinkable. But apart from the classical polis, an increasingly rare medievalism, and some nostalgia for a long-lost and more simple America, "we" have few, if any, convincing pictures of truly wholesome associations. It is also much regretted that we know so little about and do not attend enough to "the human subject." It is perhaps less true that the human subject has been slighted than that we seem to lack an applicable moral psychology. Somehow from Locke's independent learner and researcher to Freud's illusion-haunted ex-child, nothing seems quite adequate to the requirements of social theory. How much irrationality one can ignore does remain an open question, as does the whole character of the psychological and multicultural context of social thinking, especially about justice and equality. The American Scholar, and I use the Emersonian term with all its evocations quite deliberately, emerges out of and hopes for a widely shared common political order, but the incoherence of social actuality at home and abroad is such as to make such a prospect extremely difficult. This Scholar would like to say "we," not just "I," but it is not certain that philosophy permits this word, for even in its most qualified and guarded utterances it aspires to authority, not least when distributive justice is at stake. With so many groups, so many "we's," the Scholar's is but one vote among others; at best each individual speaks for one "we," not all.

How great a part does ideology play in political theory now? If we mean ideology in the strong old sense, as an explanation of social change, a setting of future goals, and a call to public organization and action, it is not much in evidence. Nor have there been any new ideologies for many years. We are not so creative in that respect as the nineteenth-century thinkers were. If, however, one simply reduces ideology to strongly held personal convictions about what is politically right and wrong, then it is obviously an important, perhaps the most important, impulse for social theory. Fanaticism will, of course, never go away, but fanaticism does not mark American scholars generally, however much their beliefs and preferences may affect their every sentence. If, however, the old continuum from left to right, from socialism to conservatism, still survives, the extremes of the old spectrum

[*15*]

are sufficiently terrifying to have set limits upon the ideological imagination. No American Scholar is eager to become an accessory to mass slaughter.

The traditions of political philosophy have continued to impose themselves on the American Scholar far more powerfully than the urges of ideology. The two names one hears most frequently are Aristotle and Locke, with Plato and Rousseau rather less often cited but hardly ignored. While in principle everyone says that the state of nature is a ridiculous fiction, it has not gone away. The reason is not hard to grasp. No one believes in Robinsonades, colonists without a past, or prepolitical peoples, but there must have been *something*, some *other* relationship among people and between people and the resources of the earth, *before* there was private property. Nothing can emerge from a void, after all. There was either communal ownership before private property was established or no possession of resources at all. Since private property is justified in terms of its origins usually, there must be a before and after. Of course one may wonder if the first person who claimed to "own" an object was even *Homo sapiens*, though that person could and did defend it against all other claims. Property may be older than we are, but history has no bearing on the question. Social logic requires an either–or choice, communal or private ownership. We left the former but may yet return to it. The state of nature remains a plausible alternative to every known historical society, and so it serves as an enduring mirror of possibilities. That is why even those scholars who reject the individualism or even "atomism" of Locke's state of nature and our fateful exit from it preserve his prepolitical myth as part of their discursive vocabulary. Locke's model human beings, independent, tolerant of differences, and seeking new knowledge as their most precious possession, is not much in evidence. They are said to have forgotten that they are the creations of their society and that their culture directs their interests and talents. Why should we, however, assume that a sense of personal self-reliance is incompatible with a full consciousness of the historical structure of any psyche? Are individualists necessarily blind to the impact of their own past and that of their particular society? It is hard to see why one should suppose so. Locke, in fact, was not naive in this respect. A strong theory of rights does not depend on historical ignorance. It does, however, require more than a mere recognition that we are the owners of our own bodies and, one might suppose, minds. For if all resources external to oneself are subject entirely to communal or governmental control, self-ownership protects one against no one and nothing. Locke may need a renewed defense, even though rights remain secure in American rhetoric and theory.

If "the great Mr. Locke" is still happily with us, Aristotle appears to be the man of the hour. He has, to be sure, been sanitized and domesticated for American purposes, but he still serves as a touchstone. It is on his authority that we are urged to think of "the human subject" not as an individual primarily, but as a social being, that is, as a part of a greater whole. We are to understand our personal characteristics and the structure of our choices and values as the expressions of a social ethos that we share and that we cannot really evade except by a flight into fantasies of perfect freedom. To be sure, we ought to forget all about Aristotle's hierarchical cosmos, his best regime, in which magnificent and magnanimous aristocrats rule and are ruled in turn while slaves do everything else, and to remember only that "human flourishing" is the object of public policy and that government must make civic education its first object. If we knew what "human flourishing" meant to all our fellow citizens, this enterprise would certainly be less problematic than in fact it is. So the suspicion that citizens must first be transformed lingers. It would be much, just now, if we could achieve an educational system that was just good enough rather than expect one that was actually good. And indeed the politics of human transformation have well-known dangers.

There is, of course, also a more modest doctrine of equilibrium in Aristotle, the chief object of which is to give both rich and poor enough honors and political powers to prevent either side from feeling so aggrieved that civil violence must break out. Balanced unequal shares for all can lead to an attenuated sense of injustice and injury and so avert the worst political evil, which is civil war. This doctrine is a great part of Aristotle's theory of distributive justice, but it is not much recalled. What we are meant to accept is the primacy of the social self and the presumed ethical harmony to which it corresponds. One may well ask what social bliss we read about in the pages of Thucydides or Aristotle, but, in any case, these struggles have little to do with twentieth-century pluralistic, multiracial, American representative democracy. The social self is useful only as an argument against those of us who think of ourselves as isolated consumers and taxpayers rather than as participating citizens or even whole human beings with an integrated communal consciousness. And it is true that fraternity does not play a conspicuous part in our lives, nor do we spend as much time deliberating about the next inter-polis war and how to pay for it as the free Athenians did. The nation-state is the source of welfare programs as well as of military policies and presumably it must be the focus of any renewed civic activity among us, remote as its government often is. The functions of ascriptive and voluntary groups can provide for some public socialization but not for a full-time political life. Moreover, it is often argued that they are just pressure groups, pushing the interests typical of a corrupt corporate semimarket society. They are, as such, not vehicles of genuine socialization. There is also a more immediate difficulty. Not everyone wants to belong to an ascriptive group. Some people prefer to be Afro-Americans, but some would just as soon be plain American citizens. Nor are all forms of association particularly conducive to human flourishing, even though voluntary and egalitarian. One ought not to forget the People's Temple too quickly.

If an expanded welfare state and greater participation in local or workplace democracy is all that redistributive justice requires, we do not really need to rethink Aristotle for practical purposes, even if it is hoped that a more communal self would emerge from such institutional changes. Who, for that matter, would not prefer to make Americans less harsh, less contemptuous of those who are ''on welfare,'' and the latter less passive or cruelly ashamed of themselves? That is, however, not a philosophical question calling for an Aristotle. Nor should we altogether forget those Aristotelians among us who are certainly faithful to the master and who insist that in principle slavery is justified and that the aristocratic regime is natural and right. To them ''human flourishing'' means the promotion of mastertypes, gentlemen of refinement, character, and wealth, and so well disposed to learning that they appreciate even the ambiguous contributions of ''the philosopher.'' As for that ''civic humanism'' which has Machiavelli as its patron saint, it has at least one advantage over all other forms of communitarianism: it champions a recognizably martial ethos, which looks upon good arms and the laws that support them as the disciplining forces for a just society. It is *not* true, however, that we have not lived through all that as an active ideology in the twentieth century.

The Left, or those who call themselves socialists, are today what Emerson called "the party of hope." Not the least of the intellectual difficulties that confront it is that communitarian and egalitarian policies may not mesh as readily as they were once thought to do. There have always been two, apparently compatible, socialist projects. One is equality through the redistribution and public ownership of all available material resources. The second is the genuine socialization of humankind. The potentially communal character of all people, everywhere, would flourish and replace the self-oriented individuals and hostile groupings of the historical past. The reeducative effect of public ownership and democracy, no less than the eventual end of material scarcities, would be transforming. There were worrying suggestions in Rousseau's state of nature and the end state of Marx's *German Ideology* that individuals freed from the division of labor might each wander off all alone, but this vision of self-sufficiency was not plausible enough for most socialists. What they looked forward to was deprivatized citizens, who could emerge only under conditions of perfect equality. It now appears, however, that redistribution may unglue rather than bond just those existing communities that would have to be the seedbeds of any socialized nation. In addition there is the recognition that if the present nation-states were to be replaced by a supranational political order, we would live under the most horrible tyranny imaginable. So both at the most local and at the most cosmopolitan level, real dangers for socialists appear to be inherent in too much redistribution. It might bring about neither peace nor humanity. One may have to settle for a more generous welfare state.

There are, of course, alternative communal visions. Long ago Benjamin Franklin organized the young artisans and journeymen of Philadelphia in clubs, "juntos," for purposes of self-education, civic improvement, political self-advancement, and social influence. Self-respect was to be the first benefit of working for paved streets. Such a citizenship is, however, as bourgeois as it is liberal, and it leaves the initiative to individuals. It is not transformative or very philosophical, but if the object is to shore up whatever communal structures remain, then it ought to be considered. It does, however, lower the sights of redistribution. And indeed there is a possibility that distributive justice may no longer be the primary goal of the "party of hope." The context of pluralism and a multiplicity of competing values distracts it. The notion of some suprapolitical agent redistributing resources without any concern for the actual conflicts of legitimate group interests or for the existing bonds of localities is unwelcome and unreal.[2] So also is the vision of a future society in which abundance and unlimited generosity render the very idea of justice superfluous, as in Plato's rational and Marx's classless orders. Somehow socialist justice and community have been uncoupled.

"The party of memory" does not have more to say for itself now than it had in Emerson's day. To lament that the classical values of Aristotle's hierarchy or Machiavelli's civic-military ethos have been ground into the dust by "the Enlightenment" is merely to say that Americans have never adhered to them. Neither has ancestor worship ever underwritten their public ethos. To summon us to return to "*the* teaching" of "*the* Founders" in the conviction that whatever was good enough for "*the* Fathers" must be good enough for us is to be irrelevant now and completely at odds with their spirit. For better or worse, they thought of America as a nation "upon experiment," and Jefferson was not alone in rejecting any intergenerational obligations. "The earth belongs in usufruct to the living: . . . the dead have neither powers nor rights over it." Even those who offer plausible accounts of the reigning beliefs of eighteenth-century Americans cannot convincingly clothe the latter in a piety that they rejected and denied. There can be nothing sacred about the past except the striving for improvement itself. Yet Americans on the Right complain of the injustices of social change. And indeed, any redistribution or alteration of social objects upsets someone's security or expectations, or threatens to do so, and this threat is always experienced as injury and deprivation. Yet conservatives also worry, inconsistently, that the energies of Americans would badly diminish under less competitive and meritocratic and therefore change-inducing conditions. Since change has indeed been our constant, in knowledge, wealth, organization, technology, ethnicity, and the character of citizenship, someone has been and must be dislocated at every moment. Why not those most able to bear social alteration?

No tradition is now more cherished than equality of opportunity. It

---

2. That is why it has been suggested that distributive justice is not a particularly viable notion in a contemporary pluralistic context. See, e.g., David Sidorsky, "Contextualism, Pluralism, and Distributive Justice," *Social Philosophy and Politics* 1 (Autumn 1983): 172–95.

is at least not a recipe for immobility and so does not recall the Founders in a manner that would have appeared grotesque to them. One might just remember their unqualified rejection of hereditary political honors, offices, and privileges and their belief in equal rights, among which opportunity came to be regarded as an important part. What sort of right is equality of opportunity? What are its claims? Is it a human or a political right? Madison, who was often concerned about social cohesion, for example, came to promote certain disruptive rights as simply necessary requirements for democratic representative government. The freedom of the press most significantly was for him not a personal but a public right, without which electoral and republican politics could not possibly flourish. If equality or opportunity is a right at all, it may be similarly public. It is expressed in the constitutional prohibition of titles of nobility, and by extension hereditary advantages and deprivations can play no part in the selection of people for offices of government or for any position requiring talent, education, or just hard work. That is what republican society is meant to be like. In fact we have come to know that the social strengths and weaknesses of family origins are not easily expunged, and that qualifications for occupational positions are socially defined. We find some of the arrangements, such as election to office, quite acceptable, others perhaps too exclusive. Clearly access to political office is defined as a public right, secured by legal procedures, and it is simply inseparable from democratic republican government. What other positions must be defined in the same way and in terms of this overriding political norm? Until we have some clear ideas about what is private and what is public, "equality of opportunity" remains undefinable. And that boundary is itself one that can be settled only by constitutionally acceptable, circumstantially conditioned decisions. It might, however, advance the discussion to realize that equal opportunity is a right by derivation, like freedom of the press, not unconditional, like that of religion and its offshoots. Thus James Madison defended freedom of the press ardently enough, but always in terms of the necessity of providing the electorate with full information about the conduct of its representatives and about the important public issues facing the nation. Before him Benjamin Franklin, himself our premier newspaperman, had recognized that although there could be no sort of governmental censorship in a free republic, some degree of self-restraint on the part of the press would be wise, since then as now papers printed gossip, entertainment, and advertisements as well as political articles. In either case, the freedom of the press is seen as an essential support of representative, constitutional government. As such it is a means to a higher end. Religious freedom is different. It is mandated by our relationship to God or by the structure of the human personality. Our very lives as moral beings are at stake in this instance, not just the best form of government for a given people at a given time, or even any time. If equality of opportunity is, like the freedom of the press, a right derived from the character of our government, its force is not at all diminished; quite the contrary. One need only consider the dangers of oligarchic, racist, and other forms of undemocratic oppression that would result from ignoring it even momentarily. Equality of opportunity also has a personally self-defensive aspect, even though its impact is radically republican.

At present equality of opportunity—or, to be exact, the right to be socially successful, if one is able—is a particular bone of contention because even those who regard economic competition as the road to dissociation, inequality, and injustice do want the benefits and flourishings that exceptional talents and just ordinary ambition may yield to their possessors and to society. A quasi-Platonic meritocracy is regarded as acceptable if "every person to do one job" allows each person to select *her* one and only role and to take *her* competitive chances, rather than to be assigned to it by public officials. The division of labor would be a matter of self-selection, especially if all basic needs were met more fully than they now are and if every person's socially recognized interests were to "matter" equally. Moreover, if monetary rewards were not pegged to the status or pleasures of occupations, then the stings of competitive failure would lose all their pains. We might even become less driven. Ambition, personal achievement, and job satisfaction, as well as all their benefits to society, would be realized with no social disruption or diminution of social cohesion. Equality of opportunity and meritocracy would in fact serve to keep society together. Still, authority would be required to share out rewards and penalties and especially status. If, in such a society, goals were shared, authority would be granted freely to the people recognized as "the best," most capable of ruling. Ambitious striving is left to the individual, in short, and the authoritative distribution of material rewards and costs to governmental authority, to "the best." If the latter considered society as a single unit, then one would end up with "work from each according to her ability as she perceives it" and pay "to each according to his needs as defined by the government." It might be a fine society, if anyone could believe that self-directed and self-advancing people would freely agree on all goals and on who "the best" were. If they did not, all the problems of distributive justice in the actual pluralistic world would also bedevil this meritocracy. To say that this would not be a democratic republic would be redundant.

There is something in the very logic of distributive justice that directs one to presuppose a uniformity of ethos. Justice as a social virtue depends on the existence of stable rules, in both its distributive and its rectifying phases. If distribution only is considered, however, a political agency that assigns shares is also implicit. It weighs and measures with a set of scales and does not have to engage in the messy bargaining of politics as an ongoing process. The judicial tribunal, not the representative assembly, is its preferred model. At worst, we get at authoritative great legislator dispensing shares in accordance with his intuitions about the local meanings of the fair and the just. Nothing in the history of political redistributions, however, suggests that this is a plausible scenario. American scholars, whether they speculate about social choices or the restructuring of opportunities, benefits, and burdens, cannot realistically forget the ambiguities of paternalism in a society such as our own, with many types of injustice as well as justice. They cannot even claim Aristotle for their patron saint. For the society that settles into an equilibrium is one of claims and counterclaims, not one happy family at all. One might argue that even rights, or claims to honors and power, can be perceived as sharing, but not as something that is handed out. These are clearly privileges that political agents acquire and sustain on their own behalf. The procedures that they may devise will benefit many of us if they are self-correcting, but not if they become simply a device for maintaining positions won once and for all. No set of institutions will, moreover, be prone to improvement and adjustment unless rights are understood as primarily freely expressed protests and refusals, not received shares. It is the defense of this sense of rights as protections that should be recalled in the midst of so many complaints about their "atomizing," "isolating," and socially debilitating, selfish character. The question at stake is: Where would we be without them?

[*23*]

It is among Aristotle's many merits that he paid as much attention to injustice and iniquity as to their more laudable opposites. The perceived sense of injustice is the main cause of revolution, and it is the chief function of the social equilibrium to impose a degree of restraint on both the rich and the poor as they work out the hostilities engendered by their respective feelings of injury and unfairness. It cannot be said that political theory has investigated unfairness and violations of the law with as much care as it has accorded justice and distribution. Unlike history and imaginative literature, it slights the cruel, the irrational, and the negative. This blandness has affected thinking about rights. It is not remembered that the history and present function of rights is the expression of personal outrage at injustice and cruelty. Rights are not a false front for impositions of power, as the Left so often claims. The call for rights is a response to very real dangers in an irrational world. And one might begin by taking the prevalence of unreason for granted. One of the causes of the present impasse of ideas about justice has been their failure to consider the sheer incoherences of social experience. To recognize these incoherences and to resort to history and fiction to illuminate them is not to sink into a romantic irrationalism or quietism. Quite the opposite, in fact. To consider the irrational is not in any way to compromise the American scholar's commitment to open and rational discourse. It is, in fact, often the most rationalist of philosophers, who are most aware of the infrangible irrationality of society, who may resort to myths, utopias, and fictions to illuminate this condition, perhaps in the hope that it may be mitigated, though sometimes in despair. Plato in the *Republic* thought that only the comradeship of military service could drag men out of their self-absorption toward some degree of social cooperation. Only organized and directed hostility, in short, could take them one step up on the ladder to reason, and many would never reach even that level. In the *Symposium* sexual love is suggested as the first slight move away from oneself, with friendship as the second ascent. It was certainly Rousseau's belief that sexual love was our first act of social self-awareness, though he often seemed to wish that we had remained stupid and limited animals rather than humans, capable of making choices, moved by active imaginations and memories. The admirers of Aristotle should, finally, recall that much of the *Ethics* is devoted to just what it is that people find so objectionable in a too limited generosity and in monopolistic political greed, and why vengeful rebellion is as usual as it is regrettable. The very existence and necessity of judicial institutions bespeaks our irrational self-regard. That is why Plato despised them. Rectification is the chief task of the fair and the just or at least of those who are institutionally constrained to be so. It is the least one can do, and far less than most of humanity can hope for.

If we take the failure of justice as our starting point, rights will not seem quite so destructive and atomistic. The stories and histories that remind us of injustice may throw some persuasive light on rights as the appeals of the injured and outraged to their all too indifferent fellow citizens or even to humanity in general. This view of rights, which has its place amid the moral and physical carnage of our age, has, moreover, a long history in America. Rights have never been demands only for more shares of whatever pie was available, nor are they inherently hostile to social conscience. Rights are demanded first and foremost out of fear of cruelty and injury from agents of governments, but also from private magnates. The former must always inspire the greatest fears because of their actual or possible military competence, but fear attaches itself to other threatening persons as well. In either case, rights are asserted against power abused.

To be heard and expressed at all, the voices calling for rights must address institutions of correction, however ineffective. If there are no open tribunals, one dare not speak. So for most people the call for rights is impossible. It has to be made by others on their behalf. For traditional oppression, revolutionary government, protracted war, military coups, and the like silence even the cry of pain. These mute appeals, like the rights demanded by the able for the incompetent— such as the calls we make for the rights of children, the sick, or the hopelessly disabled—are not like claims for legal and positive rights. They are not cases we freely pursue to restore our own rights; they are really acts of intervention to protect the most feeble from abuses. Indeed, we call them rights, perhaps metaphorically, because the word does express the fear of actual or threatened danger to all, but especially to the most feeble and helpless among us. Even when we do not protest in order to protect, but act on our own behalf by going to court to set a wrong right, to accuse, complain, and the like, we are not merely

[25]

selfish or isolating or atomistic. As Hegel most particularly noted, when one activates legal institutions, one vindicates the legal rights of all.[3] Without legality and its institutions, indeed without the simple principle of "no crime without a law, no punishment without a crime," there is no hope of any human flourishing. And while distributive justice may contemplate more in the way of fairness, it has no warrant for downgrading rights. Given the brutalities, randomness, and systematic intimidation of daily life for most people, it cannot claim that its distributions are just at all without the strictest standard of legality. "I have a right" speaks not only for "me" but for all who would protest and enjoin. It is when we look at gross injustice that rights reveal both their negative character and their far from egotistical social meaning—and their importance.

Consider the demands for human rights. What has given them such enormous urgency? The mandate of Amnesty International tells us much. It seeks the release of all "prisoners of conscience," that is, of people rotting in jail because they said or wrote something that made the agents of the government under which they live uneasy. Second, it demands fair and prompt trials for all political prisoners. Finally, it opposes all torture and executions. It calls for these rights in order to discourage governments from persecuting, torturing, abducting, and committing other acts of violence against their own citizens. Among the latter acts one ought to mention genocide, religious exterminations, and general kidnapping, although Amnesty International concentrates only on individuals. When it calls for their rights, for justice before a fair tribunal, it calls on all of us who can "to speak on behalf of those who cannot." We are summoned, in Nadine Gordimer's words, to acts of "rational empathy." We are to recognize their situation *as if* it were our own, but without ever sinking into sentimentality and the false feeling of being victimized when in fact we, the American scholars, are free and privileged in every way.[4] Nevertheless, we do ensure our own future by demanding the rights of others, for the possibility of violation is universal. The sense of injustice, which is a spontaneous reaction when we are victims, can be evoked for others, and it protects all.

3. G.W.F. Hegel, *The Philosophy of Right*, secs. 94–104, 209–29.
4. Margaret Atwood et al., *The Writer and Human Rights* (New York: Anchor, 1983), pp. 1–8, 22, 144–46.

The work of Amnesty International may look like the labor of Sisyphus as one case is instantly succeeded by others in an endless litany of horrors. It may also seem atomistic, since it works on behalf of specific individuals. We are not asked to judge these people, nor do we need to suppose that they are politically acceptable to us or part of our own community. They may eventually turn out to be no better than their tormentors. But as long as they are in jail solely because they exercised what we would call our First Amendment rights and have had none of the protections of legality, they are the victims of political injustice and usually of brutal cruelties of every kind as well. When the spotlight is thrown on them and their situation, public cruelty is dramatized in the only really effective way. For we rarely react as intensely to the plight of nameless multitudes as to the injuries suffered by an identifiable individual. The call for rights in these cases is a protest. It may encompass indirectly the inequalities of labor camps and racial discrimination, but above all it cries out directly against physical torture and illegality. In doing so it reaffirms the rights of the fortunate as well. Theories of distributive justice have relatively little to say about these matters, though we ought to remember that without political institutions of self-correction and the principle of legality, nothing can be accomplished for anyone. A too easy dismissal of rights in the interest of communal infrastructures that may ensure "human flourishing" may be an ill-conceived project in the present age.

The fear-inspired, negative, protesting notion of rights has not only present importance. It has long had its place in American political theory. A look at even a few of the more celebrated samples of political thought in that highly creative period between the Revolution and the Civil War reveals that public demands for rights as defenses against government were commonplace, and that they were not particularly self-centered or self-isolating. Indeed, there are, from the first, two distinct types of claims to rights against some established authority or other. One is directed against physical abuse; the other demands a grant or return of an entitlement or some historically guaranteed property. One is the right of the socially and politically disenfranchised, who are real or self-styled slaves, to a safe public and private life. The other is the right of real or potential proprietors—made all the more nervous by the very real presence of slavery, a word of deeper significance in America than in Europe. The former fear physical harm, the latter are afraid of dispossession. A look at that early and prophetic pamphlet by James Otis, *The Rights of the Colonies Asserted and Proved*, written as early as 1764, displays both of these impulses, one conservative, the other radically protesting. Tradition recalls the hereditary constitutional rights of Englishmen, but the rebel recognizes them as demanding a change as he insists "that the colonists, black and white, born here, are free born British subjects." That was a rare utterance, but it implied far more than a taxpayer's rights to be represented in Parliament. Both protests were meant to render disobedience legitimate, for Otis was an old-fashioned rebel who, to act, had to show that the government was aggressively endangering and injuring its subjects. The idea of a transformed future society as grounds for revolution had not yet been invented. But as he heaped imprecations upon the British, Otis also rejected enslavement in general, far removed from the ills of only his own class and city, for he protested in terms of "rights."[5]

The taxpayer's vested right as an Englishman to be represented in Parliament was certainly not unreasonable, but it was a claim to a disputed and potentially established title. Such rights were to be enshrined by John Marshall in *Fletcher* v. *Peck* as unalterable givens. Here the Georgia legislature was denied the right to revoke illegally granted land charters because "the past cannot be recalled by the most absolute power. Conveyances have been made, and those conveyances have vested legal estates."[6] This was, of course, the boldest of answers to Jefferson's belief in the primacy of the living, but it was also a vindication of rights as settled shares rather than a protest against the two basic abuses, brutality and consistent illegality, which are the real assaults on the integrity of life. Rights as entitlements are thus given precedence. Nevertheless, the two kinds of right do touch. For it is not easy to settle with any finality how much arbitrariness we are ready to accept, and for what higher ends. Philosophically it is not even clear what the relevant considerations are. It will certainly have to be something less vague than "human flourishing."

That government was the likeliest source of violence was all but universally accepted. That it was not a raging egotism to call for rights was equally clear. Thomas Paine's *Common Sense* was so enormously

5. Merrill Jensen, ed., *Pamphlets of the American Revolution* (Indianapolis: Bobbs-Merrill, 1967), p. 27.
6. Fletcher v. Peck, 6 Cranch 87 (1810).

and enduringly popular because it did indeed express common beliefs. His state of nature was not an asocial scramble but a recognizable pioneer colony held together by cooperation. Government arose in response to some inexplicable failure. Unlike society, it was not natural, and it was best treated as an unfortunate necessity, its officials to be discharged whenever they failed to satisfy. The inheritance of public authority was an absurdity best forgotten. Only elected government would do, "for where there are no distinctions there can be no superiority, perfect equality offers no temptation." It was not that Paine had no eye for social injustice, but that he thought that the days of political irrationality were numbered. That has made him sadly obsolete. But in his appeal to humane understanding, to universal feeling, to "ye that love mankind," he was hardly egocentric. Indeed, the whole idea that rights are shields against coercion is far from asocial. There is nothing particularly selfish in a call for equal rights asserted against the principle of hereditary authority. Finally, one ought to recall that the Declaration of Independence itself is a protest uttered against oppressive government. Even Madison, at one time rather less concerned than Jefferson to protect the people against their own government with a bill of rights, eventually recognized the function of rights as protest. In monarchies, he argued, bills of rights are "a signal for arousing and uniting" the community against royal force, but in a republic the danger was that the majority of the people would ignore the rights of "the smaller part of Society." This "melancholy reflection" was his answer to his older friend, who did not share those particular fears.[7] In the event, it was Madison who guided the Bill of Rights through Congress, and it is all about restraints on government ("Congress shall make no law"). Madison's fears were not ill founded, they were merely additions to the older fear of government. There was no reason to discount the awful possibility that a bill of rights might simply be ignored by majorities. His hope was that majorities might be temporary aggregations so that everyone would have the wholesome and educative experience of being in a minority with all its insecurity, and so acquire at least some forbearance. That experience is, as it were, the psychological underpinning of any effective institutional protection

7. Quoted in Marvin Meyers, ed., *The Mind of the Founder* (Indianapolis: Bobbs-Merrill, 1973), pp. 206–7.

of rights. When that support fails, as we know, the persecutive temper may well grip any community. Certainly American history has been marred and its public fiction haunted by such occurrences, and by no means only in the South. One need only think of Arthur Miller's play *The Crucible* and Shirley Jackson's story "The Lottery," both written in the McCarthy era, but both of which have survived and gained new meanings long after the events that inspired them became just bad memories.

There are, surely, always many kinds of oppression. One is an unfair government, another is a whole community that is unrestrained in its hostility to one or a few of its members. The two often go together but they are not the same. One thinks of slavery at once but there are other persecutive occasions as well that we know and can imagine. In "The Lottery" we have a village that must warm the heart of every participatory democrat. It has only slightly more than three hundred citizens and they all know each other. There appear to be no great differences of wealth or authority. Age and sex set the chief social distinctions. The coal merchant who does most of the civic jobs is childless and so has a lot of free time. People feel sorry for him. He runs the lottery with their full consent, and that consent is not forced or merely tacit. One person mentions that some places have given up lotteries altogether, but when the oldest man there says that no good comes of such departures from tradition, no one disagrees. The lots are held in a very old box that no one wants to change, but some chants and salutes that used to open the lottery have been given up. So traditions do die out. This is the old, simple, rural, cohesive America. Nothing could be more democratic than choice by lot, everyone is treated identically, even if it is a choice of who is to be stoned to death. Only when she has drawn the fatal ticket does the victim cry out, "It isn't fair, it isn't right." She now claims that her husband was not given enough time to pick his lot, but he tells her to keep quiet. It was all quite fair. What other plea, however, could she make? From a holistic point of view the rite was eminently functional. The channeling of hostilities is one way in which rituals keep societies together. These are the ties that bind. If there had been two parties, for and against the lottery, it might not have worked. It would have been divisive. It is only the victim who suddenly sees that her fate is insane, because the rest of her life is organized in terms of guilt and innocence defined by rules. Even possible punishments for crimes are set down by law here. The villagers also are insane because they do not allow their capacity for rational empathy, which their talk does reveal, to inhibit their lust for the thrill of uninhibited collective cruelty.

This is a Madisonian rather than a Jeffersonian fable. Without countervailing beliefs, preferences, human types, and other differentiations, there will be no incentives for restraint and no rational empathy. The cry "It isn't fair, it isn't right" will go up only from the victim and then too late. Matters are much less likely to come to such a pass or to last forever in representative democracies, however, than in any other regime, as Madison always remembered. It is in hierarchical societies and institutions that victimization flourishes best. The unforgettable victim-hero of Gogol's story "The Overcoat" is a humble copyist in a bureaucracy with more than thirty grades. Here there is no generosity at all. His younger, more ambitious fellow clerks torment Akaky Akakievich beyond endurance. When he finally, after many sacrifices, buys a new coat, it is stolen, criminal injury thus added to moral unfairness. The most horrible part, which destroys the poor man's will to live, is the response of his bureaucratic superior, from whom he seeks help. That Important Person, completely at sea with people only one rank below his own, screams at them, "delighted that a few words from him [can] deprive a man of his senses"; that is what he does to Akaky Akakievich, "whom no one ever thought of protecting." It is no use to say that this is tsarist Russia, after all. Every hierarchy, public and private, encourages such despotic dispositions. It is even less intelligent to say that "life is unfair," for these are not acts of an abstract life force or of lady luck. They occur when inferiors and superiors are too neatly stacked. In America slavery and its aftermath have had the same effects of blocking off all mutual identification.

Rousseau noted that kings never worried about the condition of their subjects, because they did not expect ever to share the lot of ordinary people. Harshness thus came easily to them.[8] So it does to all of us, often to the point where we forget our own vulnerabilities. The slave owners of America were particularly quick to complain of being treated like slaves when their own political rights seemed inadequate to them.

8. *Emile,* in *Oeuvres complètes de Jean-Jacques Rousseau* (Paris: Pleiade, 1969), p. 507.

Richard Hildreth, among many others, observed that "this passion for personal liberty is no where fiercer than in the hearts of an autocracy bred to its possession and who have learned to estimate its value by having constantly before their eyes the terrible contrast of servitude."[9] But their insistence on the local rather than the abstract meaning of justice made them progressively less free. The logic of their condition made them just as dependent as Rousseau had said. From nightly patrols to enforced idleness, the daily details of the planters' life were dominated by self-defensiveness, until both personal and political liberties had to be abandoned in order to secure a superiority rendered vain by the superstitions and ignorance that sustained it. By sacrificing everything to it, they lost everything in the end. The consequences of all that folly still torment a far from fair or racially sane America. For like kings vis-à-vis their subjects, whites are not likely to become blacks. Yet those slave owners did speak the language of rights—to their inherited and legally acquired property. It is only when one grasps that a human being cannot be a thing or a resource for others and forces oneself to acts of rational empathy that rights as a protest reassert their primacy. In such cases as those of the stoning and the abused clerk, the cry "It isn't fair, it isn't right" is not a claim for a share but an expression of fear, of suffering under oppression and in the face of cruelty and systematic humiliation, which we continue to inflict upon others when we can.

In that view of rights Rousseau's approach to equality may well be reworded. How much dependence, how much inequality can we bear without destroying legality and plurality?[10] Or how much equality and independence from each other do we need in order to prevent abuse and brutality on the part of governments and others who have the means of intimidation at hand? Surely Rousseau's answer, with its great legislator and underdeveloped peasantry, has nothing to say to us. In fact, there are no evident pegs on which one can hang distributive justice now. To injustice, injury, and inequality, case by case, day by day, representative democracy slowly and often quite unsuccessfully does respond. Without the procedures of constitutional government we are utterly helpless, incapable of demanding others' rights and our own.

9. Richard Hildreth, *Despotism in America* (Boston, 1854), p. 17.
10. "Tel se croit maître des autres, qui ne laisse pas d'être plus esclave qu'eux" (Rousseau, *Du contract social*, I, 2).

If effective rights require rational empathy, it is because that mental and emotional effort is the only possible psychological equivalent of John Rawls's "original position" which is historically open to us. It may not be much, but it ought to remind those who are so pleased to denounce rights and indeed liberalism generally as selfish atavisms that one might well reflect on the implications of their actual destruction and to reconsider both liberty and the conditions of liberty before abandoning them in the hope of a communitarian harmony and of social arrangements untouched by the historical experiences of our world.[11]

11. Liberty and equality are the greatest goods of all: "La liberté, parce que toute dépendence particulière est autant de force otée au corps de l'Etat; l'égalité, parce que la liberté ne peut subsister sans elle" (ibid., II, 11).

[2]

The Nature and Scope of
Distributive Justice

CHARLES TAYLOR

I

[1]

A vigorous debate is raging today about the nature of distributive justice. The controversy doesn't concern only the criteria or standards of justice, what we would have to do or be to be just; it also touches the issue of what kind of good distributive justice is. Indeed, I would argue that as the debate has progressed, it has become clearer that the solution to the first kind of question presupposes some clarification on the second. In any case, recent extremely interesting works by Michael Walzer and Michael Sandel raise fundamental questions in the second range.

I want to take up both issues in this paper. In the first part, I raise questions about the nature of distributive justice. In the second, I want to look at the actual debates about criteria which now divide our societies.

First, what kind of good, or mode of right, is distributive justice? John Rawls helps us by giving us a formulation of the circumstances

This paper has appeared in Charles Taylor, *Philosophy and the Human Sciences: Philosophical Papers 2* (Cambridge: Cambridge University Press, 1985).

of justice:[1] we have separate human beings who are nevertheless collaborating in conditions of moderate scarcity. This distinguishes it from other kinds and contexts of good. For instance, there is a mode of justice which holds between quite independent human beings, not bound together by any society or collaborative arrangement. If two nomadic tribes meet in the desert, very old and long-standing intuitions about justice tell us that it is wrong (unjust) for one to steal the flocks of the other. The principle here is very simple: we have a right to what we have. But this is not a principle of *distributive* justice, which presupposes that people are in a society together or some kind of collaborative arrangement.

Similarly we have to distinguish distributive justice from other kinds of good or right action. If in the above case one of the tribes were starving, the other would, according to a widespread moral tradition, have a natural duty to succor it; and by extension, it is usually held that the starving tribe could legitimately steal from the other if it refused to help. But acting according to this natural duty is not the same thing as acting according to justice—although the demands of natural duty can have moral repercussions on justice, as we see in the second case: the necessity in which the starving tribe finds itself and the refusal of the better off cancel what would otherwise be the injustice of the act of stealing.

Nomadic clans of herders are rather far removed from our predicament. They enter here only as exemplars of man in what is called the state of nature. The basic point is that there is no such thing as distributive justice in the state of nature. Everyone agrees with this truism; but beyond it agreement stops. The really important questions are: In what way do the principles of distributive justice differ from those of justice among independent agents (agents in the state of nature)? And what is it about human society that makes the difference?

This second question is not even recognized as a question by many thinkers. But I want to claim that it is the fundamental one. To argue or reason about distributive justice requires us to give clear formulations to strong and originally inchoate intuitions and to attempt to establish

1. John Rawls, *A Theory of Justice* (Cambridge: Belknap Press of Harvard University Press, 1971). Following Hume, I am aware of the difficulties that this formulation makes for Rawls, which Sandel has so well explored. See Michael Sandel, *Liberalism and the Limits of Justice* (Cambridge: Cambridge University Press, 1982), chap. 1.

some coherent order among these formulations. In the process, as Rawls points out in his excellent discussion of this question, both formulations and intuitions can undergo alteration, until that limiting stage where they are in "reflective equilibrium."

Now our intuitions about distributive justice are continuous with our basic moral intuitions about human beings as beings who demand a certain respect (to use one moral language among many possible ones, but it is not possible to talk about this subject at all without using *someone's* formulations). It is because people ought to be treated in a certain way, and thus enjoy a status not shared by stones and (some think also) animals, that they ought to be treated *equally* in collaborative situations (I use the term "equally" in the wide sense of Aristotle's *Ethics* V, where it includes also "proportionate equality").

If we introduce the Kantian term "dignity" as a term of art to describe this status that human beings enjoy, then it is plain that there has been widespread disagreement on what human dignity consists in. But I would like to add that this disagreement lies behind the disputes about the nature of distributive justice. We can't really get clear about these disputes without exploring the different notions of human dignity.

Now our notion of human dignity is in turn bound up with a conception of the human good, that is, our answer to the question: What is the good for human beings? What is the good human life? This question, too, is part of the background of a conception of distributive justice. Differences about justice are related to differences about the nature of the good (if I may be permitted this Aristotelian expression). And they are related in particular to a key issue, which is whether and in what way human beings can realize the good alone, or to turn it around the other way, in what way they must be part of society to be human in the full sense or to realize the human good.

The claim I am making could be put in this way: that different principles of distributive justice are related to conceptions of the human good, and in particular to different notions of individuals' dependence on society to realize the good. Thus deep disagreements about justice can be clarified only if we formulate and confront the underlying notions of the individual and society. This is the nature of the argument, and it also underlies the actual disputes we witness in our society.

The above paragraph would be a crashing truism but for two related factors. The first is the tendency of much Anglo-Saxon philosophy to shy away from any exploration of the human subject. Seventeenth-century epistemology started with an unexamined and unexaminable subject—unexaminable because any examination deals with data, and data are on the side of the known, not the knower. In a parallel way, seventeenth-century theory of natural right started with the unexamined subject. Much Anglo-Saxon philosophy seems to want to continue in this direction. Rawls is a partial exception, since he speaks of a Kantian basis for his principles of justice, expressing as they do our nature as free and equal rational beings; but even he doesn't bring this foundation out as an explicit theme. Robert Nozick is an extreme example. He argues from our current conception of individual rights, and reasons as though this conception were sufficient to build our notion of the entire social context. The question is never raised whether the affirmation of these rights is bound up with a notion of human dignity and the human good which may require a quite other context. In short, the question is never raised whether the human being is morally self-sufficient, as Locke thought, or whether perhaps Aristotle is not right about this matter. An argument that abstracts from this conception, and that is insensitive to the social nature of human beings, naturally produces the most bizarre consequences.

I really want to argue here for an Aristotelian way of putting the issue about distributive justice. But Aristotle not only has a substantive view about man as *zoon politikon* which conflicts with Locke. He also has an implicit metaview (a view about what is at stake in the argument). And this view conflicts with that of a philosophical tradition of which Locke is one of the patrons, which wants to make questions of human nature irrelevant to morals and political philosophy, and to start instead with rights. This means that it is, alas, not just platitudinous to restate Aristotle's way of putting the issue. A second reason for reediting Aristotle naturally follows: the precise way in which different notions of distributive justice are related to their foundation in a view of human beings needs to be restated.

The Aristotlelian metaview I want to put forward here is that principles of distributive justice are related to some notion of the good which is sustained or realized or sought in the association concerned. We can illustrate this view first with a very un-Aristotelian theory, the atomist view of Locke. For the purposes of this discussion we can describe as ''atomist'' views of the human good in which it is conceivable for an individual to attain it alone. On these views, in other words, what people derive from association in realizing the good are a set of aids only contingently, even if almost unfailingly, linked to this association; protection against attack from others, for example, or the benefits of higher production. Such benefits always require association, or almost always. But there are imaginable circumstances in which we could enjoy security or a high living standard alone; on a continent in which there were no others, for example, or in a land of paradisiac natural abundance.

A social view of the human good, by contrast, holds that an essential constitutive condition of the search for it is bound up with being in society. Thus if I argue that an individual cannot even be a moral subject, and thus a candidate for the realization of the human good, outside of a community of language and mutual discourse about the good and bad, just and unjust, I am rejecting all atomist views, since what a person derives from society is not some aid in realizing his or her good but the very possibility of being an agent seeking that good. (The Aristotelian resonances in the above sentence are, of course, not coincidental.)

To put the issue in other terms, social views see some form of society as essentially bound up with human dignity, since outside of society the very potentiality to realize that wherein this dignity consists is undermined; whereas atomist views see human dignity as quite independent of society—which is why they have no difficulty ascribing *rights* (as against just the status of being an object of respect) to a person alone, in the state of nature.

Now the issue of the principles of justice is quite differently posed within these two views. For the atomist, there is such a thing as the aims of society, that is, purposes that society fulfills for individuals, who are morally self-sufficient in the sense that they are capable of framing these purposes outside of society. Thus Locke's thesis that "the great and chief end of men's entering into commonwealths is the preservation of their property" is posed against the background that individuals acquire property outside of society by mixing their labor with it "without the consent or assignation of anyone."

But outside of society, human beings are in the predicament of our nomad tribes above; and the rules of justice that prevail are not those of distributive justice but those of independent possession. Conse-

[*38*]

quently, an atomist view gives one the basis to argue that what we have a right to under these original rules cannot be abrogated, since the purpose of entering society cannot be to jeopardize these rules but rather to protect them. And from this reasoning one can derive an absolute right to property, which no society can infringe.

What, then, does entering society change? What does it add to original justice in the specific form of distributive justice? This depends on the aims of the association. Let us take Locke's aims as our example. The aim of the association is to preserve property, which of course includes life, liberty, and estate. But if all enter into society freely, then all should benefit from the association. This is the basis of a principle of equality, the principle of equal fulfillment, that is, the principle that society's aims should be equally fulfilled for each of its members; for otherwise some in joining would be giving more than they got, would be sacrificing themselves for others; and there is no reason why they should do this (outside of a special context in which a natural duty might come into play, as when someone is starving).

In the Lockean case, the principle of equal fulfillment requires that the government protect equally effectively the life, liberty, and estate of each of its subjects. Of course, this equality only not is compatible with but one might argue even requires inequality of another sort, since the state would have to protect the legitimately arrived-at distribution of property, no matter how unequal that distribution was. (And on some plausible thesis about the hazards of many transactions, the distribution couldn't help being unequal, as Nozick argues.) But this would still be equality of equal *fulfillment* of the aims of the association, and hence would be justice.

We thus see two kinds of arguments for principles of distributive justice which are apposite in an atomist perspective. The first invokes the contextless justice of the state of nature and argues for the (partial) preservation in civil society of some of its features. This is the basis for one of the arguments for inalienable rights. It can also be seen as the basis for Nozick's entitlement theory of justice, where all that enters into account is the series of permissible transactions between independent agents.

But one might object that this is not a principle of distributive justice at all, which becomes relevant when people are associated together in society and have to share in some sense. Now it can be argued that

[*39*]

the underlying notion of distributive justice is equality, that people associated together for the good have to share in some way in this good, or else a wrong is being done. (The notion of equality here is Aristotle's of *Ethics* V, as I mentioned above.) But the question is: What is the relevant kind of equality? And here an atomist view can give us an answer by invoking the aims of the association. The fundamental notion of equality as basic to distributive justice is interpreted here to mean that there should be equal fulfillment. So that what equality means in society is directly dependent on what are seen to be the aims of the association; for equality is just the fulfilling of these aims for everyone alike.

These two kinds of argument, on the other hand, have no weight in the perspective that sees human beings as social animals. Rather two other kinds of argument are invoked which offer only a distant parallel to the atomist ones.

First, any social view sees a certain kind or structure of society as an essential condition of human potentiality, be it the polis or the classless society or the hierarchical society under God and king or any other of the host of social structures that we have seen in history. This structure itself, or order, or type of relation, thus provides the essential background for any principles of distributive justice.

This means, of course, that the structure itself cannot be called into question in the name of distributive justice. Within the bounds of a hierarchical conception of society in which the political order is thought to reflect the order in the universe, it makes no sense to object to the special "status" or "privileges" of king or priest as violations of equality. When this objection is made, it involves a challenge to the entire hierarchical conception.

This point is generally recognized, and might be thought to be of no relevance to our age. But although such hierarchical conceptions belong now to an irrevocable past, the underlying form of argument does not. For if we have a conception of a certain structure that is essential for human potentiality, or for the fullness of human potentiality, it defines for us the kinds of subject to whom distributive justice is due. It is not just that the normative structure is untouchable, but also that it is between persons-within-the-normative-structure that justice must be done.

To take an example from a peripheral discussion of John Rawls's book: in Section 77 he takes up briefly the question whether a real equality of opportunity wouldn't have to equalize the advantages people derive from their family backgrounds. Obviously, there is a potential thrust to the argument for individual equality which, taken to its limit, would have us break up families, perhaps even bring children up in state institutions, in order to bring about true equality of condition. Why do we shrink from this? Because we have the intuition that growing up in a family is linked with an important aspect of the human potential; or to use the ancient language, that forming and living in families is "natural" to us. To those who think this way, the argument that we should break up families in order to do justice between individuals seems absurd. The absurdity arises from the sense that the proposed breakup would no longer be doing justice between full human beings but between truncated people. So that the very ground for justice as equality, that it is bound up with the respect due to human dignity, would give way under the argument.

But of course this idea that families are natural to human beings can be challenged; and naturally it is challenged by the more extreme offshoots of the modern tradition of "absolute freedom," such as some variants of contemporary "women's liberation." From this point of view, the family is an imposture, an oppressive structure masquerading as a natural form. And we have an argument parallel to that around the hierarchical society of the ancien régime.

We can take another example that brings us to a more central dispute in modern Western polities. Within some general agreement (at least avowed agreement) that the life chances of people in different regions and classes ought to be equalized, there is an important disagreement as to what this means. For some people regional equalization means that where the economically most efficient solution is to encourage out-migration, one take this most efficient route to the goal of equality between *individuals*. For others, on the contrary, it means bringing about comparable living standards for the different regional societies, as *communities*.

Of course, like all political disputes, this one is fought out in all sorts of terms, and it may even be that some philosophical confusion is essential to achieving political victory. It is nevertheless true that one of the underlying issues is this: Is living in the kind of community that one sees, for example, in Cape Breton Island or the Gaspé Peninsula essential to (an important) human potential? If so, then equality must be between people-in-such-communities, and this means we must adopt the second solution. But if, on the contrary, we look on this sense of community belonging as simply a taste that some people have, then there is no reason why it should be subsidized by the rest of the society; our duty is rather to take the cheapest road toward equal living standards for individuals. To spend more resources refloating the economy of a region so that it need not suffer out-migration is then to give people in the disfavored regions *more* than their due.

(Of course, in politics you have to muddy the waters. Those of us who are in favor of the second policy *also* argue that it is the overall cheapest, particularly because of the cost of writing off the stock of houses, schools, etc. in the declining areas. We can't afford to ignore the atomist vote. But our philosophical grounds aren't revealed in these [we hope politically persuasive] arguments.)

From a social perspective there is a first kind of argument, therefore, which spells out the background against which the principles of distributive justice must operate. There is no comparable notion of background on an atomist view. Or, if one wants to discover one, the nearest thing to it would be the state of nature, the original predicament of justice between independent beings, where justice is not yet distributive justice.

But this kind of argument can generate its own parallel to the notion of inalienable rights: types of relationships that human beings should be able to enter into and remain in, and that cannot be normatively overridden by other considerations such as distributive justice.

In the above examples I have spoken of the background as being set by certain considerations about the human good or potentiality as such good. But this is perhaps an overessentialistic and certainly a too restrictive perspective. The framework for distribution can also be determined for a given society by the nature of the goods its members seek in common. It can vary historically.

I could, for instance, have put the second example above in these terms. One could make the claim that equalization ought to be between regional communities, because the nature and purpose of the association in question (here the Canadian federal union) was to secure the health and flourishing of its constituent regional communities. We could prescind altogether from issues of human (transhistorical) nature whether human beings are by essence community animals; we would just argue that the very nature of the common good defining our association precludes our conceiving equalization in purely individual terms.

Michael Walzer's brilliant *Spheres of Justice* offers a whole series of arguments purporting to show the justified distribution of different goods that we in a certain sense produce or provide in common, reasoning in each case from the nature of the good provided and the character of the agents who have associated for its provision.[2] Thus he argues that the character of the universal citizen self-rule that has become central to modern Western democracies renders illegitimate the exercise of essentially political power that is based on the ownership of property (chaps. 4 and 12). This argument justifies a condemnation of the famous Pullman experiment, but also, he thinks, tells in favor of workers' control at least of large-scale economic units.

Again, he argues for certain principles governing the provision of welfare—especially that goods be distributed in proportion to need and that the distribution recognize the underlying equality of membership (chap. 3, p. 84)—on the basis of the nature of the goods and our common understanding of membership in a democratic society. Analogous arguments are put forward for a redistribution of the burdens of hard and dirty work, involving even a republican version of the corvée (chap. 6).

Now what all these examples have in common is that they involve a fixing either of the forms and structures of distribution (e.g., that goods should be partitioned between people-in-families as against people-as-individuals) or of the actual shape of the distribution (e.g., welfare should be provided according to need), from considerations of human good or the nature of association as such, or at least from a consideration of the particular goods sought in a historical association. There is no question as yet of the differential merit or desert of the members. Rather arguments of the kind I have been considering here purport to set the framework in which considerations of desert can be allowed to arise, if they are allowed to arise at all, and determine distributions. The framework ought to be given priority over other criteria of distribution because whatever transgresses its limits would

2. Michael Walzer, *Spheres of Justice: A Defense of Pluralism and Equality* (New York: Basic Books, 1984).

[*43*]

allegedly be in violation of the nature of the goods distributed or of the agents to whom they are distributed. And to propose an allocation of this kind in the name of distributive justice has to be absurd.

The second form of argument that arises in a social perspective concerns the principles of distributive justice themselves, and not just the framework. Granted a certain view of a common good, in the sense of an indivisible good, which a social perspective necessarily offers us, since it sees human beings as realizing their potential only in a certain common structure, it may appear evident that certain people deserve more than others, in the sense that their contribution to this common good is more marked, or more important.

We could put it this way: For this common good of living in a family or a community or whatever, we are all in each other's debt. But we might see the balance of mutual indebtedness as not entirely reciprocal. Some people, those who contribute in some special way to the animation of the community or to the common deliberative life of the society or to the defense of its integrity or whatever, deserve more, because we are more in their debt than vice versa.

This is the perspective of Aristotle's discussion of distributive justice in Books III and IV of the *Politics*. He closely links together what the principle of distribution of offices and honors ought to be and what the common good is which the polis is for.

Now in Aristotle's society, particularly given the importance of honor and its position as one of the key goods at stake in the issue of who could have a political career, this type of argument was naturally used to justify certain inequalities (or as Aristotle put it, certain "proportionate" equalities). But the argument form can serve also as a ground for equality, and does in the modern world. For it can be used to rebut the claims for unequal distribution based on some other criterion, say economic contribution. The argument here runs along these lines, that although individuals' economic contribution to a society may be of very unequal value, nevertheless, as members of a community who sustain together certain kinds of relations, of civility or mutual respect or common deliberation, their mutual indebtedness is fully reciprocal, or sufficiently reciprocal so that judgments would be impossible and invidious. We shall return to this consideration below.

This second type of argument can be applied in two different ways, both of which we find in Aristotle. The first way, illustrated in the preceding paragraph, is to hold that because of a common good that in fact is sustained by the common life of our society, we ought to accept certain principles of distribution that take account of the real balance of mutual indebtedness relative to this good. For instance, that we owe each other much more equal distribution than we might otherwise agree to on economic criteria, because in fact we are involved in a society of mutual respect, or common deliberation, and this is the condition for all of us to realize together an important human potential.

Or we can apply it in another way: recognizing that a certain kind of society, such as one of common deliberation in mutual respect, represents the highest realization of human potential, we might judge that certain or most societies have not yet arrived at the point where this ideal is fully embodied in their common life. If this is so, then for certain societies that are still far from the best it would be wrong to apply the principles of justice that belong to the best. Thus if a society is in fact much more fragmented than the ideal of common deliberation, much closer (at its best, that is, freed of the savagery and exploitation it may contain) to a society of mutual protection, whether because of its history, its mode of economic life, its cultural diversity, or whatever, then it may be wrong to demand, say, the degree of equality that we can justify between those in a true community of common deliberation.

Of course, we would still consider the latter to be a better society, and try to move our society closer to that goal. And we will probably judge our society harshly for all sorts of injustices that are unjust on its own terms. But it may nevertheless be wrong to demand in the name of justice a standard of equality from this society unchanged which we would think normal and enjoined on us in the best society. We may judge, for instance, that the tenuous relation of semi-alliance between two cultural groups in a state does not justify the equal sharing of all benefits and burdens that is indispensable in the polis.

We can thus see two kinds of argument in the social perspective, paralleling the two kinds of argument in the atomist perspective. The first, as it were, sets the framework for the principles of distributive justice apart from the notion of the common good which we are involved in. The latter tries to derive these principles from this same notion.

There are limit cases of social perspectives in which the second argument is lacking altogether. These are cases in which, once the structural demands for the common good are met, there is no further room for questions of distribution. The two most famous cases that are (it can be argued) of this kind are the views of Plato and Marx. To take the latter case, this may help explain what many people have found rather odd, that there seems to be no doctrine of distributive justice chez Marx. This can be explained, I believe, by the fact that the conception of the communist society in which alone the human potential is fully realized contains a principle of distribution (to each according to need) as a structural feature, essential to it as community. So that all questions of distribution are decided by the framework argument. There is no room left for arguments that we recognize as being properly about distributive justice, that group A or group B deserves or merits more or the same, in virtue of the balance of mutual indebtedness. A parallel argument might be made in the case of Plato.

What is interesting in the highly original work of Michael Walzer is that he seems to be attempting a similar feat but in an infinitely more supple and pluralistic fashion than either Plato or Marx. By a similar feat I mean a theory that will determine all the questions normally thrown up for distributive justice by considerations of the framework type, without recourse to questions of desert, or what I have called the balance of indebtedness. The principles are of course utterly different from the Procrustean one we see in Plato. Indeed, the theory is in a sense the ultimate anti-Procrustean social theory; and this, I believe, is what is tremendously valuable in it. But the question may still arise whether one can do altogether without any principles of distributive justice in the narrow, intraframework sense. It is not that Walzer is trying to tie down the distribution of every good by some antecedent criterion. On the contrary, the whole thrust of the work is to limit the scope of distributive criteria to their proper domains. It is just that where distributions are not determined by some framework considerations, they are left quite unrestricted. The market is an example. Its operations have to be restricted at certain places in the name of other goods; but within its legitimate scope the allocations brought about through it are legitimate without being deserved. People are entitled to what they get, but there is no place for considerations of desert or the balance of mutual indebtedness in determining, say, incomes policy.

[46]

[2]

What emerges out of the above discussion is above all two major points about the nature and scope of distributive justice, confusion about which bedevils discussions today. The confusions arise from conflating distributive justice with other virtues, so that it is no longer clear just what is being demanded or advocated. This is not a merely "academic" question, as I hope to show; rather the confusions may hide from us important political choices.

1. Aristotle, in distinguishing particular from general justice, points out that the former is a virtue whose opposite is "pleonexia," grasping more than one's share. Criteria of distributive justice are meant to give us the basis for knowing what our share is, and therefore when we are being grasping. But what falls out of the above discussion is that there are two rather different kinds of argument that do this. There are arguments about the nature of the framework, from considerations of the goods sought and the nature of the agents associated; and on these grounds we sometimes judge that certain distributions are wrong and that those who push for them are "grasping." And then there are arguments about the balance of mutual indebtedness which justify some distributions within the framework and rule out others.

Both of these arguments concern distributive justice in a sense; but in another sense, only the latter do so, because only they tell us how to resolve questions of distribution that can be considered as open and allowable questions in the light of the framework. They help us decide the distributive questions that we can legitimately allow as questions without subverting the good or the very basis of our association. However, the issue of how to use the term is not vital, so long as these two levels are not confused.

2. Both framework questions and the criteria of distribution are derived at least in part from the nature of the association and that of the goods sought in common. But that means that the demands of distributive justice can and will differ across different societies and at different moments in history. This is a crucial point that is hammered home effectively in Walzer's book, for instance. As a matter of fact, the variation may take us beyond the range of distributive justice altogether, as Michael Sandel has shown in his penetrating work. Certain associations—families, for instance—may be such that the presumption

[47]

of independent interests implicit in demanding distribution by entitlement may be destructive. The good of these associations may exclude distributive justice.[3]

But even if we restrict ourselves to those societies where some form of distributive justice is appropriate, it is clear that they may be widely different; and even that some may require principles of justice that are wrong—principles that we can even call unjust in another sense. The fight between Agamemnon and Achilles over Briseis is a dispute about distributive justice. Both parties justify their behavior in terms of a principle. (Achilles holds that she is part of his share; Agamemnon holds that the ruler can't be left with less than the followers.) Let's say only one of them is right in terms of Mycenean warrior society. Nevertheless, as far as we're concerned, people shouldn't be allocated in this way, as spoils of war.

If we ask why we think so, we will recur to the discussion above about the atomist perspective. We believe that there are some ways we should and shouldn't treat each other quite irrespective of whether we are associated together in society or not. In the state of nature, people shouldn't treat others as booty. This is unjust, in a sense that has nothing to do with distributive justice within a society. The fact that we see the social perspective is necessary to raise questions of distributive justice doesn't mean that we cease to believe in certain inalienable rights. The error of atomist writers like Nozick was to try to make the right of this asocial context the *sufficient* basis for distributive justice in society, which it can never be. But avoiding this error doesn't mean that we abandon all transsocietal criteria of right.

So we can say that Briseis is justly Achilles' (let's side with him); but the whole operation is unconscionable and wrong. In less dramatic fashion, we might consider some society in which the degree of solidarity is morally inferior to another; or one in which the goods sought are defined in a narrowly material fashion, excluding the cultural development of the members. Certain distributions may then be just in terms of the society but repugnant to us.

This suggests that it might be important to distinguish the society we attack specifically for failing in distributive justice from the society we see as failing in absolute justice (to use this term for the good violated in the Mycenean case) or some other good. Nor would this

3. Sandel, *Liberalism and the Limits of Justice*, chap. 1.

distinction be necessarily a purely pedantic exercise. To try to make a society more distributively just is to try to make it conform more to the constitutive understandings shared among its membership. To try to make a society absolutely just, or bring it closer to absolute justice or some other good, may well be to subvert and destroy the constitutive understandings. Agamemnon and Achilles would have to be totally reeducated, their economy and way of life largely abolished, before they could renounce what we find utterly unacceptable in their conduct. But there are costs, sometimes terrible costs, in such transformations, as is evident to us once the hold of imperialist politics and atomistic philosophy on us weakens.

This means that revolutionary critics of injustice can be in a political dilemma: should they break altogether with the regnant standards of distributive justice, in order to bring people up to a higher type of association, more in line with the good or with absolute justice, but then risk the dangers of deracination, the breakdown of civility, the debilitating effect of whatever vanguard tutelage is necessary, and the like; or should they respect the dominant culture, even at the cost of renouncing the higher good? There can, of course, be no simple answer to this dilemma. In cases where slavery and ritual murder are involved, we might easily agree to take the revolutionary road; while with a society that failed to some degree with regard to solidarity and a concern for the better things of life, we might more readily feel bound to work within.

A dilemma of this kind might be thought to exist for us now, at least in principle, in the international arena. We might argue that the present distribution of the world's resources between rich and very poor is scandalously unjust, judged by the standards of absolute justice we acknowledge in the state of nature. No one would be right to leave another in such need should they meet in the desert, for instance. And yet the degree of sacrifice that would have to be imposed on rich countries to effect the required transfers might be impossible short of despotism. International justice might be uncombinable with democratic rule in the developed countries. Absolute justice here would require that one violate distributive justice in these polities, and indeed, smash the present matrices in which existing standards of distributive justice have grown.

I think we also face this dilemma in more immediate and less dramatic forms in our societies, as may be indicated in the sequel. But much of the contemporary discussion about distributive justice ignores its very possibility. It could be argued that Rawls, for instance, is presenting us with a highly revisionary standard of justice in his difference principle. I shall try to show that this is so below. But the question whether it is can't even arise as long as one sees the task of defining the principles of justice as an ahistorical one, a single question to be asked and answered for all societies irrespective of their culture and traditions and self-understandings.

II

[1]

After this long discussion of the nature of the argument, I want to look at the issues about distributive justice that are current today. There are two areas in which these issues constantly arise. One is that of "differentials," the question of the allowable differences between wages or income received for different kinds of work. This is becoming a particularly acute question as Western societies find themselves experimenting with incomes policy more and more.

The second major area is one that we can designate roughly as equalization policies. This rubric covers the whole gamut of policies that attempt in some way to redistribute income or economic prosperity or life opportunities, either by transfer payments or by special programs to develop certain regions or to allow certain disfavored groups to catch up in one way or another (e.g., in opportunity for education). These policies are the object of sometimes bitter controversy today, and one that gets to the heart of the issues about distributive justice.

In both of these spheres the issue is equality, and it might be schematically introduced in the following way: Equality is a powerful ideal in Western society just because we have put behind us all views of society as embodying some kind of differential order, views that formerly justified unbridgeable differences of status. There are no longer any reasons in the order of things why one group should perpetually and systematically have a different lot than another.

At the same time the growth of technology and the modern industrial economy has given us (the sense of) unprecedented power to alter our natural and social condition at will. So that not only the ancient class inequalities based on the "order of things" are no longer justifiable, but also other inequalities, such as those between regions, which used to seem just inevitable and beyond remedy. Now, for instance, the difference in standard of living between southern Italy and the rest of Europe is seen not just as a consequence of the hazards of history and natural endowment but as a problem to be solved. The same goes for other pockets of poverty within favored regions, which were formerly thought of as unalterable.

All this means that there is a growing pressure toward equality, a growing impatience with long-standing and stubborn gaps in living standards. This on one hand. But on the other hand, there is a powerful resistance to equalization. This needs no special explanation; when have the comparatively better off *liked* redistribution? Nevertheless, the resistance takes place in a certain climate, which has important consequences. Western industrial society, having done much to break up the old local communities that were previously important in people's lives, has brought about a "privatization" of life. By this I mean here a generally accepted picture of happiness and the good life as that of a person alone, or more exactly, a nuclear family alone. The promise of greater control over nature which our civilization holds out is naturally translated in this context into a promise of increased individual control, which means having disposition over an increasing number of individual consumer goods. The aspiration to perpetually rising consumer standards has become very powerful in all Western societies.

Privatization naturally makes us tend to look at society as a set of necessary instruments rather than as the locus in which we can develop our most important potential. This is by no means the only way we look at it, but it is an important part of many people's consciousness of society. And privatization tends to be self-reinforcing, since a society whose institutions are seen mainly in instrumental terms is one that offers very few intrinsic satisfactions and that people naturally tend to withdraw from whenever feasible to their own private space. This tendency is well illustrated by the fate of modern cities, whose cores become progressively less agreeable places to be, with a consequent flight to the suburbs, which in turn . . . and so on.

All this is well known and much commented on. Its relevance for the discussion here is that these conditions ensure a continued vogue to atomist views. In a way it might seem strange that in such an unprecedentedly interdependent society, where we are farther away than ever from the original human condition of self-subsistent clans, people should still think in such atomist terms. Locke might be excused for such a view, in a still largely agricultural society, and even more the framers of the American Republic in the late eighteenth century. But how can such views survive today?

In a sense, of course, they don't. No one can believe the fables about a state of nature. But in our moral reasoning these atomist views do survive, because the experience of so many people in modern society is one that atomist views seem to make sense of. Not that it is ever conceivable that we might have put society together from scratch, but rather that society and its institutions are seen as having only instrumental significance; that what we need to acquire the full range of human purposes we already possess as individuals, or develop in close, intimate relations with others, while the larger society merely provides us with the means to carry them out (while also, alas, putting obstacles in our way).

Hence we find atomist forms of reasoning about distributive justice which have a certain currency. Of course, the original Lockean form seems not too plausible to most people in modern society. On this view, human beings already had outside of society an independent capacity to exploit the resources of nature, and their so doing (mixing their labor with nature) founded property. This kind of myth about property is still important in some parts of the United States for historical reasons. But it obviously has no relevance to the life experience of the vast majority in Western society, which is rather that of working within large and complex structures.

But there is another starting point for an atomist view which is the individual not as possessor of property but as an independent being with his or her own capacities and goals. The aims of association are here not so much the protection of property but the combination of our capacities, which allows each of us to be much more productive than we would be alone. Our capacities, what we bring to the association, are, however, of very unequal value. Thus on the principle of equal fulfillment of the aims of association, those of us with especially useful capacities, and who really use them to the full in our collaboration with others, ought to receive a greater share of the resultant product.

[52]

This is not a doctrine that is anywhere spelled out. Rather what I am trying to do in the preceding paragraph is sketch what I think is the implicit background to a widely held principle of distributive justice in our society, which we can call the contribution principle. This is (at least partly) what lies behind the widely felt intuition that highly talented people ought to be paid more than the ordinary, that professions requiring high skill and extensive training should be more highly remunerated, and in general that complete equality of income, or distribution according to need, would be wrong.

Of course, there are many other reasons why people oppose equality of income, one of the principal ones being the sense that it would dry up the stream of outstanding contributions. But I am trying to account for the intuition not just that such equality might be disastrous but that it would be *unjust*, and this is based on what I have called the contribution principle. It matters not at all that in fact the task of applying the contribution principle with certainty, of assessing the real relative value of the contributions of doctors, lawyers, orchestra conductors, garbage collectors, welders, ship pilots, and so on, would be next to impossible; that any solution requires countless arbitrary stipulations. What matters here is that people have an intuition about relative values at least in "obvious" cases (surgeons vs. garbage collectors, for instance), and this alleged difference of contribution justifies differential remuneration.

If we take the underlying reasoning of the contribution principle, it is evident that some differentials are just on the principle of equal fulfillment, and it may even appear that equal payment would be a kind of denial of an "inalienable" right, treating me as though my exceptional capacity were not my own, but in some way belonged to society. But I identify with this capacity, and feel expropriated in my being. (For a parallel type of reflection, see Nozick's discussion of the equivalence between taxation for transfer payments and forced labor.)

There is great strain in many Western societies between the drive for equality on one hand and the sense of justified differentials which the contribution principle yields on the other. On one side it is felt that in a highly interdependent society, whose arrangements can be remade virtually at will (this sense of omnipotence is probably illusory, but that's another matter), the less favored have a justified sense of grievance. On the other side, as the measures designed to redress these inequalities become more expensive (and they include not only transfer payments but also programs designed to develop regions and classes, as well as certain universal programs), the middle classes, or in some cases the affluent in general, see their aspiration to continually rising consumer standards being jeopardized. But the redistributive measures seem to be in favor of the less endowed and the less hard-working. And since our contribution is a joint function of capacity and effort, massive redistribution violates the contribution principle. The affluent now have a sense of justified grievance.

If we take these two perspectives alone, there is no reason why the tension shouldn't build up almost indefinitely, until continued democratic politics become impossible. But Western society has managed to stave off any such reckoning in the postwar period by sustained rapid growth. Growth enabled them to meet the higher demands of public expenditure to redress the most politically pressing inequalities and provide certain services universally (the pressure for the latter type of program came of course also from the middle classes) and at the same time to ensure rising consumer standards to the affluent. Now that continued growth is becoming more difficult, tensions are beginning to rise. Uruguay may provide a terrifying preview of the fate of many Western polities.

As the tension builds up, the sense of grievance on both sides increases, and the sense of society as having a legitimate claim on our allegiance or making legitimate demands of social discipline declines. From both sides, the "system" comes to seem irrational and unjust. When the unskilled see how the doctors are able to command a large increase in already (to them) astronomical incomes, they conclude that the operative principle of distribution is according to blackmail power. This feeling is intensified when they discover the tax concessions that the middle class and the self-employed can often take advantage of. But from the other perspective, these increases and these concessions are seen as an all too grudging recognition of superior contribution, enterprise, and effort. On the contrary, from the standpoint of these privileged people, their just differential is constantly being eroded by excessive taxation, because politicians succumb to the power of the mass vote.

So on both sides there grows the sense of being imposed on by sheer force, and the principles of justice invoked seem sham. This kind of belief is, of course, self-fulfilling, in that feeling the victims of force, people respond with force, and so on in a spiral. A reasoned debate about distributive justice becomes impossible.

This impossibility is all the greater if the sense of being imposed on by force finds expression in a coherent belief. For instance, the Marxist belief that capitalism systematically distorts and frustrates human potential and that it can only live on exploitation entails the view that there is no valid answer to the question "What is just?" within the purview of capitalist society. It is irremediably a domain of force. There is no point in even discussing the "right" differentials; the whole system has to be brought down. From this point of view, no incomes policy can be the right one; all have to be sabotaged.

[2]

How can a philosopher enter this debate? Presumably by setting out a well-grounded criterion of distributive justice. John Rawls's book, one might think, provides an outstanding example of this enterprise. But the burden of the above argument is that it is not so simple. A well-grounded principle would have to spell out one of the above background arguments; and if we set aside atomist views as illusory, we would have to spell out a view of the indivisible good bound up with social life as part of the indispensable background to a principle of justice, as well as the foundation for the principle.

Rawls does something somewhat different. He develops a more exact specification of the principles of justice by means of the imaginative detour of the contract argument. This strategy is supposed to enable us, by invoking rational choice theory, to arrive at a more exact formulation of the principles. But the contract argument doesn't offer us the reasons for believing that these are the right principles. It isn't itself an argument of any of the four kinds above, and in particular, it isn't an atomist argument. On the contrary, Rawls's rejection of what he calls a "private society," one where the institutions are merely instrumental to private purposes (in sec. 79), shows how far he is from the atomist tradition of Locke.

Rawls's difference principle is in fact highly egalitarian; I mean relative to the present society in the West. This may not be immediately evident for two reasons. First because a number of academics have criticized it from a Marxist perspective, some variants of Marxism being quite popular in the contemporary academy. But Marxism, as we saw, makes a totally egalitarian society part of the basic structure, so that there is no more room at all for a principle of distributive justice. Thus any principle that allows that there might be some grounds for justified unequal distribution of ultimate satisfaction (it is this satisfaction, of course, and not goods, that is equally distributed on the Marxist criterion; "to each according to his need" may mean that I get more *goods* than you if my need is greater), however mitigated and minor, would be unacceptable from a Marxist point of view.

The second reason for misunderstanding is that there are some difficulties in actually applying the difference principle, and we might confuse it with the "principle" of blackmail that actually seems to operate in a number of Western societies, whereby privileged groups giving an indispensable service drive the hardest bargain. But this is plainly not Rawls's intention. If we set this aside, and compare the difference principle not with some perfect Marxist society but with the contemporary reality, it is clearly a departure in an egalitarian direction, specifically in that it is a challenge that "no one deserves his greater natural capacity nor merits a more favorable starting place in society" (102), and states that "the difference principle represents . . . an agreement to regard the distribution of natural talents as a common asset and to share in the benefits of this distribution whatever it turns out to be" (101). This "socialization" of our capacities is directly contrary to the view of the individual and society which underlies the contribution principle.

Broadly speaking, there seem to be three main families of views about distributive justice in our society. Starting from the "right," they are the contribution principle (I ignore the even farther right Lockean atomism that sees an inalienable right to property, since this view is found virtually nowhere but in the United States, and even there is not a very powerful one); the family of liberal or social-democratic views that justify egalitarian redistribution; and Marxist views, which refuse the issue of distributive justice altogether on the grounds that the question is insoluble here and unnecessary in a communist society. Rawls's view falls plainly in the second category.

But then enunciating the difference principle isn't enough; or even deriving it from a calculation about contractors in the original position.

We have to justify it by a background conception of human potential and the human social condition. Nor must we do so just in order to make the difference principle persuasive to protagonists of other views. We need to clarify the background in order also to see whether this principle is an appropriate one to invoke in our society. For in discussing the Aristotelian framework for arguments about distributive justice above, I pointed out that the derivation of the principles of justice from a notion of the common good can work in two ways. We can attempt to show that because of the common good that is in fact sustained by our society, our principles of justice ought to change; or we may come to accept that because of the limited common good that we in fact manage to sustain, the principles apposite in the best society cannot apply to us.

I see Rawls's difference principle (and his two principles in general) as the principles apposite in the best society. I recognize there is something a little presumptuous about this, since I am seeing Rawls's argument through an Aristotelian prism that he doesn't accept. The distinction he makes is between the general theory of justice and partial compliance theories, which is not the same as Aristotle's reasoning about justice in less than perfect states. Nevertheless, I don't think there is too much strain in seeing these principles as the ones that would be appropriate in the best state, in view of Rawls's discussion in the third part of the book, where we see how they could be an integral feature of a truly just and humane society.

If we ask what is the background notion of the individual and the social good which underlies Rawls's principles, the answer is that we can't find it directly in the book, because Rawls doesn't think this way. But there are passages of direct argument for his views (as against argument that passes through the contract detour), as for example the one cited above (sec. 17, discussing equality). And if I may be once again extremely presumptuous, I should say that the vision of the good society in section 79, as the social union of social unions, in fact is what underpins Rawls's principles. If this Humboldtian vision is correct about the nature of our mutual involvement in society and the kind of common good we sustain, then (a) equal liberty is an essential background feature of society (and hence has priority) and (b) we ought to accept a far-reaching equality, well beyond the contribution principle.

Supporters of the contribution principle, however, will not be satisfied with this. They will question whether our actual society bears any relation to the vision of a social union of social unions, whether they are not being asked to buy a principle of equality that would be apposite in a quite different world. This is a tough question, not easy to answer; but it cannot be assumed away.

However, I cannot continue the discussion in connection with Rawls; I have already presumed enough in attributing to him answers to questions that he didn't put. The point of the above was only to show that, if my understanding of the logic of the argument for distributive justice is right, simply giving such a clear and elegant formulation of an egalitarian principle can only be the beginning. The hard part of the answer is yet to come.

But there is another way in which it seems wrong to give any single coherent set of principles as the criteria of distributive justice. And that is that our reality itself is many-sided, and more than one argument is valid. To see this it would perhaps be best to start with a skeletal version of the arguments that are relevant today; and this is what I'd like to do for the next paragraphs.

We could start with a critical examination of the atomist mode of thought that underlies the more pugnacious affirmations of the contribution principle. In fact, however understandable atomist views may be in the light of modern social experience, they are all illusory. First of all, the talented individual who makes a valuable contribution owes much of his or her capacity to society. It is not just that the training without which this capacity could not flourish is often provided by the larger society, but also that the very fact that someone with this capacity can make a large contribution may depend on a given mode of economy or social life. Someone with great mathematical gifts is much in demand in an age of computers, not at all perhaps in prescientific society. Such a "contribution" there is of no account. Similarly, a person with a gift for rhetoric has something to give in a society where there is much litigation and public persuasion, as in the ancient polis or contemporary democracy; but this talent may be much less important elsewhere. The very concept of "my" contribution needs to be further examined.

But what is more fundamentally wrong with the contribution principle is the error of all atomisms, that it fails to take account of the degree to which free individuals with their own goals and aspirations, whose just rewards it is trying to protect, are themselves possible only within a certain kind of civilization; that it took a long development of certain institutions and practices, of the rule of law, of rules of equal respect, of habits of common deliberation, of common association, of cultural self-development, and so on, to produce the modern individual; and that without these institutions and practices the very sense of oneself as an individual in the modern meaning of the term would atrophy.

Atomist thought tends to assume that the individual needs society, democratic institutions, the rule of law, only for the Lockean purpose of *protection*; the underlying idea being that my understanding of myself as an individual, my sense that I have my own aspirations to fulfill, my own pattern of life which I must freely choose—in short, the self-definition of modern individualism—is something given. In a sense, if I look only at this instant of time, there is some truth in this idea, since the conditions of civilization that have helped to bring this situation about are already behind me. I have now developed the identity of an individual, and a fascist coup tomorrow would not deprive me of it, only of the liberty to act it out in full. Indeed, once this identity has developed, it is hard to stamp it out, as modern tyrannical regimes have discovered.

But over time this identity would be reduced if the conditions that sustain it were to be suppressed: first of all, by the impossibility of continued free interchange with others, which nourishes our sense of our own goals; second, by the loss of responsibility for the direction of public affairs, without which our moral reflection on these affairs would tend to lose the seriousness of deliberation over real options (although the story of Soviet dissidents shows that a minority will never lose this).

Under conditions of prolonged tyranny, individualism for the majority of the succeeding generations would become something quite different: a sense of one's private tastes, a world of relationships cut off from the public world, a great desire to be left alone by the powers whoever they be. And even here one's tastes might be severely limited by the cultural proscriptions imposed by the powers.

For some atomists this might be sufficient as a sense of the individual; all that would be missing would be liberty to act it out. But if we follow the tradition of Montesquieu, Tocqueville, Humboldt, and J. S. Mill in seeing it as a truncated version of the aspiration to liberty, then something follows for the theory of justice. For we have not only to maintain those practices and institutions that *protect* liberty but also those that sustain the *sense* of liberty. For this is to accept the (social) perspective that the very potential for the good (here liberty) is bound up with a certain form of society.

To the extent that we think of ourselves as already formed by the past development of these institutions and practices, our obligation to maintain them springs from a principle of justice between generations, the conviction that the good we have received we should pass on. This idea has an important effect on the principles of justice we will accept. If we think of the public institutions as just existing to protect liberty, they can consist with almost any degree of inequality, as we can see from Locke's theory. But if we think of these institutions as nourishing the sense of liberty, and in particular through interchange and common deliberation, then great inequalities are unacceptable. This point has been continually made in that branch of the modern liberal democratic tradition which was inspired by ancient republics; we can see it, for instance, in Montesquieu, Rousseau, and Tocqueville.

If we see ourselves as engaged together in a society that not only defends liberty but also sustains the sense of liberty, then the two forms of argument of the social perspective become relevant. First, a certain degree of equality is essential if people are to be *citizens* of the same state, and so this degree of equality becomes a background feature that any principle of distributive justice must conform to. And second, it can be argued that the balance of the debt we mutually owe as citizens, maintaining together institutions of common deliberation, is much more equal than is that of our economic contribution.

Hence we can see that undermining the atomism that underpins the pure contribution principle also ends up at least severely limiting this principle. For first, the inequalities that it might generate have to be mitigated by the necessary background conditions of a society sustaining liberty; and second, they are offset by another quite independent criterion of desert. This not to mention the effect of the earlier arguments cited above, to the effect that our contribution is not entirely ''ours,'' since both our developed capacities and their value owe something to society. This consideration must modify the effect of the contribution principle toward an egalitarian direction.

But does it do away with it altogether? Have we found in the conception of a society sustaining liberty the single source of a coherent set of criteria of distributive justice? If we think so, then we will argue for a highly egalitarian society. Indeed, it would be difficult to argue for any inequalities at all, except for those that might be allowed by the difference principle, which are precisely such as don't cost anyone else anything. Or they might allow for inequalities of a noneconomic sort: a just distribution of honor in a republic can never be egalitarian; indeed, honor equally bestowed (unlike respect) is not honor; and some people will arise who serve the society sustaining freedom in an outstanding way; they deserve honor. (These considerations are, of course, squarely in the ancient republican tradition.)

It would be tempting to argue in this way, particularly for those modern socialists who are nourished on the tradition I have just mentioned. But the protagonists of the contribution principle could protest that it was wrong, on exactly the grounds mentioned above, that it assumes a society we have not yet got.

Defenders of a mitigated contribution principle could argue that although we have indeed a society that aims to sustain liberty, this is not the only good we seek in society. We are not citizens of an ancient polis with our lives entirely focused on Montesquieuan *vertu* or Hegelian *Sittlichkeit*. For us society is *also* valuable as a collaborative enterprise whereby the contribution of each can be multiplied through coordinated activity. Consequently, the atomist perspective is not just an error; it corresponds to one dimension of our social experience.

In other words, on this view, our contemporary society is such that it cannot be understood within the bounds of a single theory. It has aspects of the republic in it, sustaining liberty, as well as of the collaborative enterprise serving private purposes. This complexity, or plurality of focus, becomes the more evident when we reflect that the boundaries of society for one or another purpose are not necessarily the same, and are indeed perhaps not altogether clear.

As collaborators in an economy, we are linked together in one sense with virtually the whole human race, now that the world economy has penetrated virtually everywhere. That is why there are certain questions of distributive justice that arise internationally (as against the obvious issues of retributive justice, where restoration is due for plunder, rapine, conquest, spoliation, etc.). So that our obligations by the contribution principle may go beyond the boundaries of our political society.

By contrast it may be argued that in certain cases the community within which we sustain our sense of liberty, personality, individuality is smaller than our political society. This may be most palpably the case in multicultural societies. But an analogous point might even be made in homogeneous but large societies. At least it might be argued that the more intense or culturally vital relations of a local community give rise to more far-reaching obligations of distributive justice. The level of equality one can demand, for instance, might be more far-reaching within a local community than between such communities.

What all this means is that we have to abandon the search for a single set of principles of distributive justice. A modern society can be seen under different, mutually irreducible perspectives, and consequently can be judged by independent, mutually irreducible principles of distributive justice. Complexity is further compounded when we reflect that there is no single answer to the question of the unit within which people owe each other distributive justice; that even within one model of society, there are different degrees of mutual involvement which create different degrees of mutual obligation. So that we may have to think of justice both between individuals and between communities, and perhaps within communities as well.

If this all means that there may be no such thing as *the* coherent set of principles of distributive justice for a modern society, we should not be distressed. The same plurality emerges in Aristotle's discussion of justice in *Politics* III and IV. Those who adopt a single exclusive principle, Aristotle says, "speak of a part of justice only" (*meros ti tou dikaiou legousi*, 1281a10).

[3]

This complexity need not reduce us to silence, but it means that there are no mathematical proofs in regard to distributive justice. Rather the judgment of what is just in a particular society involves combining mutually irreducible principles in a weighting that is appropriate for the particular society, given its history, economy, degree of integration. It is hard to set out knock-down proofs of such judgments.

But some things can be said in general about Western societies. All or most are or aspire to be republican societies that sustain the sense of individual liberty and common deliberation; and at the same time all or most are also experienced by their members as collaborative enterprises for the furtherance of individual prosperity. The first aspect is the basis for a principle of equal sharing, the second for what I have called the contribution principle. (This latter, incidentally, can be separated from its illusory atomist mode and put in a social perspective: one of the goods sought in common is prosperity, and in relation to prosperity the balance of mutual indebtedness is not strictly reciprocal, since some people make bigger contributions than others, and thus *as far as this criterion is concerned* deserve greater shares.)

Justice involves giving appropriate weight to both of these principles. And this means, on one hand, that we cannot envisage a society of completely equal shares, that is, one in which the contribution principle would have no place, unless we can alter our society very fundamentally in a socialist direction. And this means not just toward public ownership of the means of production, which could after all be introduced just as a more effective and/or fair way of encompassing everyone's (individual) prosperity (and this is how it is ending up in Eastern Europe, whose societies are no closer to equality of income than ours). It would mean a society in which the major good sought by the majority in engaging in economic activity was no longer individual prosperity, but, for example, some public goal, or the intrinsic satisfaction of the work itself; or else a society where people's needs were few and limited, and where production for the means to life had no interest beyond a certain modest level of prosperity, but where all surplus energies were devoted to other things, that is, the kind of society of which the ancients talked and Rousseau dreamed. In such a society, people would seek a greater share of honor, or of public office (which Aristotle lists as the major goods about whose distribution justice is concerned), and would be less concerned with a greater share of income or wealth.

In short, it would take some major institutional-cum-cultural change in our society, so that one of the major goods sought in common was not individual prosperity, for the contribution principle to cease to be a valid principle of distribution of income. Of course, strictly speaking, in any society that is *inter alia* an enterprise of economic collaboration, and that is any society outside of Arcadia, and in which the economic contributions are not equal, as they cannot be in an advanced technological society, some form of the contribution principle is valid. But in some society that had undergone one of the cultural mutations referred to above, where individual prosperity was not the principal goal, signal

[*63*]

contribution would entitle one to something other than greater income; public honor, for example, or more meaningful work, or perhaps greater leisure, or sabbatical leaves (the intellectual's dream).

But if the contribution principle seems irremovable prior to such a transformation, it remains generally true on the other hand that it is invoked in an obsessive and one-sided way in our societies. Because of the privatizing features of our culture mentioned above, atomist illusions continually arise, that is, there is a tendency to forget the ways in which we depend on society to be full human agents, and also to be capable of the contribution we are making. Taking account of these considerations would require that the contribution principle be combined with three other, more egalitarian ones.

The first, as mentioned above, is the requirement of what we can call for short a republican society, where a common citizenship requires a certain degree of equality, or to put it negatively, cannot consist with too great inequalities. This is the background condition. The second consideration, also mentioned above, is the principle of distribution that arises out of our republican society, and in which the balance of mutual indebtedness is much more equal, except insofar as some who make a signal contribution to public life deserve special consideration.

The third arises from the negative arguments against the atomist contribution principle which I adumbrated above, to the effect that our contribution is not entirely "ours," since both the forming of our capacities and their worth depend to some extent on society and its modes of production.

[4]

What does all this tell us about the politics of distributive justice in our societies? There are in fact two major directions in which one can go if one accepts the argument so far. The first is to take the principle of equality implicit in our society qua republican and seek to transform our society so that it can be integrally carried out. This means undertaking one of the transformations mentioned above. The Marxist vision of the classless society offers one such, but there are others, such as the ideal of a commune life based on limited needs in some balance with nature. And there are more. In most cases the incentive to pursue these revolutionary changes is strengthened by the belief that the present structures are corrupt or distorted or contradictory to the point where there is no valid answer to the question of distributive justice as things stand. But in one way or another, the goal is held up of a society that would be beyond the contribution principle and could thus be a fully equal society.

The other major road would be to accept that some version of a contribution principle society is here to stay, and concentrate rather on making the other three considerations palpable enough to the society at large so that equalization measures will be readily accepted. This is the politics of the majority Left in a great many Western countries today.

Income differentials are thought to be justified to some degree by the contribution principle; and then alongside these differentials, equalization measures are taken: certain minima are assured to everyone, for example, in virtue of being a member of a republican society; measures are taken following the principle of redress/development to help poorer regions.

The difficulty today is that neither of these roads seems satisfactory. The first banks on a transformation of culture and aspirations which is too far-reaching to hope for. But the second runs into the fact that the two principles of modern societies, let us call them for short the contribution and the republican principles, are in great and increasing tension, as I discussed in the first section. The privatizing features of modern culture, which include greater mobility, the decline of traditional communities, the growth of the megalopolis, the pressures of consumer society (itself partly a result of privatization), tend to give rise to an atomist consciousness, and make people less aware of or make them have less belief in the republican dimension of our society. The growth of large-scale, highly interdependent, bureaucratically run, big-city societies is exercising the destructive, alienating effect on our republican life which the writers of the tradition always predicted.

The result may be that the two principles will be pitched against each other, that is, they will cease to be recognized as necessarily complementary for our society; but each will be put forward exclusively and will see in the other a pure exercise of force (the blackmail power of those with indispensable skill on one hand, the naked, leveling force of the mass vote on the other). Strangely enough, for this to happen we don't even need society to divide into two mutually exclusive groups.

[*65*]

The astounding thing is how many people, while being ambivalent and invoking now one, now the other of the major principles, nevertheless interpret each in its exclusive, polemical form; affluent workers, for example, indignant about "welfare bums" (a real myth bred by the contribution principle, since studies show that the amount of cheating on the welfare system or on unemployment insurance is not great at all) on one hand, and about the excessive increases in doctors' incomes, or even in those of other sorts of skilled workers, or else various middle-class tax concessions, on the other. Societies can break up because people develop a general sense of being systematically "ripped off," even if this conviction isn't based on a single consistent principle.

The result of this radical polarization would be a society in which atomist illusions would grow apace while feeding in the opposite camp unreal dreams of transformation to an equal society; while on both sides there would be an overwhelming sense of living in a society where mere force or political muscle but not justice makes the law. In this kind of society policies of true distributive justice become impossible politically, and they become above all unrecognizable as just by any of the parties. And indeed, at a certain point in the decay of a republic into the rule of force or tyranny, the question may arise whether the very basis of any principle of distributive justice, which is association for the good, has not been undermined. Argentinians and Uruguayans may be asking this question today. Let us hope we won't be asking them tomorrow.

It will of course be very hard to offset the drive to bigness and concentration, and the associated drive to growth. But if we are to avoid the scenario just described, we may have to do something of this sort. I have discussed this circumstance elsewhere in connection with Canadian politics, but it is hard to define policies on a general level, since each Western society has a peculiar situation and history. In general, however, it would seem that we have to move toward some decentralization of decisions and planning, which will mean that some of the smaller communities that make up the larger modern polity will have to be strengthened or revived. Second, we may have to turn away from such an exclusive concentration on rising consumer standards, the major expression and underpinning of contemporary atomism.

Ten years ago changes in either of these directions would have seemed politically impossible. But now other factors—the decay of

[66]

large urban concentrations, the rising costs of public services, the fact that we are encountering the limits to growth—may help to force us in these two directions. That is, if they do not precipitate even faster the breakup of republican society described earlier. In the end these two outcomes—the move toward a more decentralized society, less totally focused on growth, on the one hand, and the slide toward tyranny on the other—may be the major alternatives we face.

If this is so, then neither of the roads described above is adequate. The choice will not be between revolution to take us away from the contribution principle altogether and modest reform in order to bring it into balance with the republican principle; rather we may need fairly far-reaching change simply to retain or recover this balance. The changes will probably be far-reaching in two senses, not only in the general goals and aspirations but institutionally as well. It is highly likely that we cannot expect to have a society that is more decentralized and less addicted to growth without breaking the economic hegemony over many Western societies of the large corporation (or the multinational corporation, to express it in the terms that the issue takes in Canada). We need a radical socialist politics stripped of the traditional utopian socialist illusions. But this alternative may be too weak in face of the illusions of atomist self-dependence on one side and the Marxist mirage of communist society on the other, which both draw on the favorite self-delusion of western civilization, that of absolute freedom.

[3]

Rousseau on the Equality of the Sexes

ALLAN BLOOM

I

There are people in Europe who, confounding the diverse attributes of the sexes, claim that they make man and woman beings not only equal but alike. They give to both the same functions, impose the same duties on them, and accord the same rights to them. They mix them together in all things, work, pleasures, and business. It is easy to grasp that in this attempt thus to level the sexes, both are degraded. . . . This is not the way the Americans have understood the kind of democratic equality that can be established between man and woman.

. . . if I were asked to what I think the singular prosperity and growing strength of [the American] people ought to be primarily attributed, I would respond that it is to the superiority of its women.

These two passages from Tocqueville's *Democracy in America*[1] summarize the questions to be addressed in this essay: What effect does the principle of equality have on the relation between the sexes? That

This paper is based entirely on Alexis de Tocqueville, *Democracy in America*, trans. Henry Reeve, rev. Francis Bowen (New York: Vintage Books, 1945), especially vol.2, pt. 3, chaps. 8–12, pp. 202–25; and Jean-Jacques Rousseau, *Emile*, trans. Allan Bloom (New York: Basic Books, 1979), especially IV and V, pp. 221–480; with occasional reference to Plato, *Republic*, V, and Rousseau, *Politics and the Arts: Letter to M. d'Alembert on the Theatre*, trans. Allan Bloom (Ithaca: Cornell University Press, 1968).

1. Tocqueville, *Democracy in America*, vol. 2, pt. 3, chap. 12, pp. 222, 225; translation mine.

principle, according to Tocqueville and his teacher in these matters, Rousseau, is *the* principle of justice and the foundation of the only legitimate form of political regime, democracy. The true knowledge of equality and its incorporation in the real lives of human beings are modern phenomena, and the early thinkers who provided the intellectual foundations of democracy reflected profoundly on the meaning and the consequences of this one political absolute.

At the origins, equality was understood to be the principle of nature as opposed to the conventional order in which some men ruled others by pretended right of strength, wealth, tradition, or age. The relations of king and subject, master and slave, lord and vassal, patrician and pleb, rich and poor, were revealed to be purely manmade and hence not morally binding apart from the consent of the parties to them. Civil society was to be reconstructed on the natural ground of its members' common humanity. Consent became the only source of political legitimacy. It would appear from this perspective that all relationships or relatedness depend on the free consent of individuals. Inevitably, political right and the understanding of nature connected with it affected the view of relationships within civil society which are less doubtfully natural and less arguably conventional than those just mentioned, that is, those between man and woman, parent and child. They cannot be interpreted simply as the result of acts of human freedom and seem to constrain that freedom. If they are natural absolutes, they seem to give witness against the free arrangements of consent dominant in the political order. But if they are to be understood as are other contractual relationships, they lose their character and dissolve. It is difficult to argue that nature does and does not prescribe relatedness at one and the same time. The radical transformation of the relations between men and women and parents and children was the inevitable consequence of the success of the new political dispensation. In just what way they would be transformed and what the reflexive effect of the transformation on the political order would be became Rousseau's central concerns. He presented the issue as the core of a crisis of modernity and democracy.

Prior to Rousseau, it might be said with some exaggeration, the teachers of equality paid little attention to men and women and the family. They concentrated on the political order and seemed to suppose that the subpolitical units would remain largely unaffected. But there are two different understandings of nature present here, one in which nature has nothing to say about relationships and rank order and another in which nature is prescriptive. Are the relations between men and women and parents and children determined by natural impulse or are they the products of choice and consent? The former view is part and parcel of ancient political philosophy, as one easily sees in Aristotle's *Politics* I, whereas the latter view is at least implicit in Hobbes's and Locke's state of nature. The common teaching of the political philosophers has always been that the political regime will inform its parts. Hence democratic politics will produce democratic sexual and family relations. But what are they?

In *Emile* Rousseau addressed this question more comprehensively than anyone had done before or has done since, and it is to a few reflections on this enormously influential but now largely forgotten book that I shall limit myself, in the belief that Rousseau, because of his privileged position at the beginnings of modern democracy, saw the problems with special clarity and intransigence, and that, however unpalatable his views have since become, he both played an important and unsuspected part in forming our views and is especially helpful if one wishes to get a perspective on our peculiar form of wishful thinking.

II

To begin where we are at, the moral and perhaps even the political scene has been dominated for two decades by two movements, sexual liberation and feminism. Both have somehow to do with the status of sexual differentiation or "roles," and both are explicitly connected with the extension and radicalization of egalitarianism. The two are not necessarily harmonious—witness the squabbles over pornography—but each probably presupposes the other, and they represent aspects of the struggle to adjust free individuality to the demands of our sexual nature. Rousseau foresaw both as necessary consequences of liberal theory and practice and was strongly against them. His reasons for this stance are of little concern to his contemporary critics who are committed to liberation and feminism, and he is now probably the archvillain of sexual politics. He is qualified as a guilt-ridden puritan by one camp and as a sexist by the other, and is subjected to the indignities of psychological interpretation. His continuing good reputation in other quarters is attributable to his powerful advocacy of community, which is all the rage. But that his treatment of sex can be explained only by his concern for the conditions of community—conditions that were, according to him, rapidly disappearing—is hardly mentioned. Rousseau's dedication to the cause of close communitarian ties between free and equal men and women forced him to pay the closest attention to that most powerful motive, sex, which joins and separates men and women.

Puritan he surely was not. He was one of the most powerful critics of the notion of original sin, and insisted on the natural goodness of man, especially of his sexual desire. It is a common error to treat opponents of sexual liberation as though their only ground were theological, whereas it is possible to limit sexual gratification for economic, social, and political reasons and even in the name of good sex or love. Rousseau wished to liberate sex from its theological yoke in order to consider its delicate relationship to all the powers of the soul. If sexism means insistence on essential differentiation of function between man and woman both naturally and socially, then Rousseau was indeed a sexist. If, on the other hand, it means treating women as objects and subordinating them, he certainly was not a sexist. Rather he was concerned with enhancing the power of women over men. Beginning from the community of man and woman in the act of procreation, he attempts to extend it throughout the whole of life. Procreation is not incidental to life but, properly elaborated, is the end, that for the sake of which all things are done. It is the relatedness, the harmonious relatedness of man and woman, which he takes as the model and foundation of all human relatedness.

Because modern political theory and practice begin from the rights of individuals "to life, liberty, and the pursuit of property," the dangers of egoism (read "narcissism" today), of a constricting of the soul within the limits of the individual and material I, and hence of a diminution of man, are, according to Rousseau, great. Liberal democracy, unless its characteristic springs of action are complemented or sublimated, would not then be a simply choiceworthy regime, even though it were founded on just principles. Rousseau discerned in man's historical experience three great loves that could draw him out of his selfish concerns and solicit his soul on the highest level—love of God, love of country, love of woman. Each is an enthusiasm, even a fanaticism, the objects of which are made unique and beyond purchase by the activity of imagination. The operations of the first two have been rendered nugatory, or at least have been radically attenuated, by modern philosophy itself, which had as one of its primary goals the destruction of fanaticism. Tocqueville summarizes Rousseau's observations about patriotism and religion in an egalitarian age: Attachment to country is a calculated judgment, not a passion, and religion is largely a moral teaching intended to put a damper on materialism. Neither has the character of an end in itself or a consummation, the proper domain of the noble or the heroic. Religious authority is undermined by reason, and government becomes the protector of private rights, not the school of public virtue. Fanaticism is, Rousseau and Tocqueville agree, a cruel and sanguinary disposition, an enemy of reason and of peace. But it is also frequently the cause of a self-forgetting and dedication absent in preservative and economic motives. It displays generosity and splendor. It is possessed of a poetic charm not present in dreary commercialism. The immediate consequence seen by Rousseau is that the love between man and woman must be preserved and encouraged, for it is the politically undangerous fanaticism that ennobles human beings and can, by way of the family, even strengthen the political order. It can be thought to be natural and healthy in a fuller sense than the other two, because it has a bodily base and a bodily fulfillment in sex. The further consequence is that sexual liberation, as opposed to religious and political liberation, must be combated in order to avoid the demystification of love, as God and country have been demystified. As faith had become superstition and fatherland the state, so love would become sex, and there would be nothing left to oppose the atomizing tendencies of egalitarianism. Love means the directedness of the two sexes to one another and their complementarity, so that a true unity can be achieved instead of the contractual and conditional connection of two like and selfish individuals.

As a consequence of such reflections, Rousseau put eroticism at the center of his thought, and these reflections provide the answer to the question of the unity of his writings, which appear to be divided between public and private, political and romantic works. The defectiveness of politics requires the supplement of love, and eros as the proper realm of imagination, idealism, and beauty reveals itself only by the demystification of the theological and political realms. What at first glance seems to be a disaster—the coming into being of that which Rousseau was the first to call "bourgeois" society—turns out to provide the opportunity to gain clarity on the human situation and to separate out its elements so that they may be harmoniously reordered. Thus the new political science, which was intended to be self-sufficient, was father to a new science of morals and a new aesthetics—noble interpretations of equality and freedom—providing for the full development of the human faculties. The sentimentality, romanticism, and idealism of Rousseau, which so infuriate latter-day Enlightenment rationalists and seem so far from the coolness and sobriety of Locke, are merely the result of thinking Locke through, especially the latter's comparative neglect or downplaying of sex and imagination. They must be given their due for the sake of preserving the political order and avoiding the impoverishment of man.

Hence Rousseau's novelistic works, *Emile, La Nouvelle Héloïse*, and *Confessions*—each of which is much longer than his primary political treatises, the two *Discourses* and the *Social Contract*, put together—constitute an attempt to establish what was missing in earlier democratic thinkers, a democratic art. He does for democracy what Socrates did for aristocracy in the *Republic*. The artistic need—which Rousseau understood to be related to the religious need—was unsatisfied in liberalism, with the attendant risk of either philistinism or the persistence of the influence of artistic forms and models drawn from the old tradition—biblical or Plutarchian—inappropriate to democratic life. Democracy requires democratic taste, for taste, much more than abstract principle, determines way of life and choice of pleasures and pains. There is the closest of links between taste and morals. In his *Letter to M. d'Alembert on the Theater* Rousseau criticizes the aristocratic and urban character of the theater as well as its bloated heroes, whose example has nothing to do with the lives democratic men lead. The novel, in the establishment of which as *the* literary form in an egalitarian age Rousseau played a leading part, is better suited to democratic men. It is cheap and accessible everywhere, does not presuppose extensive and fixed periods of leisure, does not require participation in a public ritual where wealth and rank are on display, and is therefore not as necessarily allied with vanity and snobbism. Its personages can be people more like ourselves. The tedium of the daily life of democratic man, with its lack of splendid actions, can more appropriately find its

[*73*]

place in a novel, and the cultivation of the private life and private sentiments are more satisfactorily depicted in it than on the stage. The joys of rusticity, the presence of nature, and the attachments of family belong especially to the novel. Good novels can be the constant, life-interpreting companions of men and women in regimes where communal sharing in the sublime has all but disappeared.

And the central theme of Rousseau's novels is the relations between men and women—love, marriage, children. *La Nouvelle Héloïse* is the archetype of the romantic novel; and *Emile*, the prototype of the *Bildungsroman*, is nothing but the education of a husband. One does not often imagine that the thoughts of Hobbes, Spinoza, Locke, and Hume were primarily occupied with sexual relations. Rousseau was the first of the modern philosophers to return to Plato's concern with eros. And the connection between this concern and art is evident. The love of the beautiful unites them. The early modern thinkers put their emphasis on fear of death as the fundamental motivation, and it is an individuating passion as well as one that looks to the ugliness of man's situation. The coupling passion becomes secondary if the passion that isolates the self is more powerful. The world that is devoted to avoiding death or providing comfortable preservation is prosaic. Rousseau was attempting to restore the Platonic eros for the beautiful on new grounds and, if not to render the world poetic again, at least to embellish its prose. The sexual fantasy and the perfect partner that it envisages is the natural base from which he begins.

Thus, when Tocqueville says that American women are the cause of the American success, he means that the attachments to them formed by American men were of the kind that would support American institutions. These were strong, austere, and modest women who did not flinch from the life of pioneers, who did not demand great luxuries, and who practiced and demanded fidelity in marriage and were dedicated to their children. They were, at least in Tocqueville's interpretation, the principle of the family, which gave men a goal beyond their individual selves, which involved their daily thoughts and feelings, an end for the sake of which their hard labors were performed. The family is a unit intermediate between individual and society and provides a link between them. America was a nation of families—perhaps themselves composed of individuals, but individuals whose *choice* of family gave them interests, in both senses of the word, different from those of raw individuals. This is so simply because in the family the self is passionately expanded in space and time. The family man must care in an unconditional way for other individuals as well as himself, and he has an inevitable commitment to the future extending beyond his own life. Wife and children are not the only possible motives of such spiritual expansiveness. But in an egalitarian society the others (Tocqueville suggests that among them are politics, religion, art, and philosophy) are not readily available, nor are they so natural, gentle, or easy. The political order that serves families is very different from the one that serves individuals, if the latter is even possible. When the society is not an educator of citizens, the family can at least provide persons who are open to the demands of the large community because they care for a small community that is their own. It is thus the directedness of a man's sexual desire to a woman of a certain kind that is the foundation of the family. Tocqueville accepts Rousseau's maxim, which Rousseau took from Plato, "Do you want to know men? Study women." In every nation they have reciprocal characters, and there is no political solution unless there is a sexual solution.

III

Men and women have to adapt themselves to one another because they must get sexual satisfaction and civilized human beings want willing partners. Traditionally, since it was women who put up the resistance and had to approve those who were attracted to them, men had to do and be what was necessary to gain a woman's consent. If women were promiscuous and lived in the atmosphere of a court, a man had to be of a different kind to succeed with them from the one who would appeal to chaste women desirous of a rustic and domestic life. The inner difference here can be measured by the distance between seduction and courtship. Whatever a man's public responsibilities or work, a large part of his most intimate private life, taste, and fantasy is involved with his sexual relations (unless sex is trivialized and made meaningless) and the demands his partners make on his character. If the two sides of his life do not cohere, both public and private suffer and regimes change. The private pleasures win out in the long run. Plato suggested that the austere, public-spirited Spartans secretly longed for voluptuous sexual satisfactions to which their lascivious women tempted them. Therefore Spartan virtue was forced and founded on repression rather than on love of virtue. The almost impossible task of harmonizing the public demands on the male warriors with what their attractions to women inclined them toward led Plato, or rather his Socrates in the *Republic*, to innovate and give women the same education and the same work as men. All the elements of liberation with which we are so familiar are found there—day-care centers, birth control, abortion, equal access to athletic facilities, along with less familiar items such as infanticide and nudity in common exercises. Sexual differentiation disappears and has no more significance than does the difference between the bald and the hairy. But this is done not in the name of women's rights but of what is needful for the community. Socrates simply abolishes women, and hence the division of labor between men and women which does not match the city's economic and political division of labor. The private pleasures and the private family to which the difference between the sexes point cannot be conciliated with full community or communism. In Socrates' city what unites human beings of either sex is the overriding common good and nothing less. Reproduction becomes an incidental aspect of life, one that does not affect its goals, and education of the young is entirely public. There is left no tension between public and private. Women represent privacy, in pleasure, property, and family. They have to be separated from their children if all children are to be treated equally.

Rousseau's analysis begins from Plato. He does not dispute the desirability of total dedication to and involvement with the community. Morality means self-overcoming in favor of the common good. His disagreement with Plato is about the natural desirability of the political order. Men care naturally about themselves in the first place, and Spartan civic virtue requires a "denaturing" of man both difficult to achieve and harsh on individuals. National attachment is both fanatic and abstract; there is no natural impulse toward the large community, which requires myths—that is, lies—to be believable and the rewards of which are honor and glory, imaginary and dangerous will-o'-the-wisps. Such a city is achieved at the cost of the sweetest natural pleasures—erotic satisfactions—and their associated natural sentiments, love of men and women for one another and love of children. The differences between the two kinds of relatedness is measured by the contrast between the overwhelming and also questionable passions of Plutarch's heroes, which make them capable of their political sacrifices, and the gentler, more common, and more effective motives for sacrifices on the part of men and women in love, and parents, the persons depicted in Tolstoy's novels, for example. Rousseau puts family where Plato put city, as the end for which other things are done and as the ground of relationships, partly because he lowered standards and expectations, partly because he saw in the former greater humanity.

If Plato's civil promiscuity, the completely utilitarian treatment of sexual intercourse, were to persist when the city was no longer the highest goal for its citizens, total individualism would result. What was done away with for the sake of the city was what was necessary for the family. A rational division of labor that does not take account of sex is possible. The separation of men and women and the psychological inhibitions that went with it hampered such a rational division of labor. Male and female went the way of aristocrat and commoner, native-born and foreign-born, and so on as a distinction that is not pertinent to the jobs to be done. But what determines the jobs to be done now? The market. A person must make himself over to fit whatever jobs are created by the impersonal forces of the market. No longer is the adaptation arguably to natural requirements, such as those of the city or the family. Ruler, warrior, and priest can be said to perform functions always politically necessary and even fulfillments of human potential, as is also the case of mother and father in the family. But riveter or computer programmer are just jobs, related to what is produced, not to the fulfillment of the human potential. Thus the individual is utterly alienated to the market and its ever-changing demands, his or her existence defined by it. And it is pure, anonymous, becoming. These observations of Rousseau form the kernel of Marx's critique of capitalism and its effect on the family. Man, woman, and child are categories that impede the growth of capital. Capitalism is interested only in workers, and feminism is but bourgeois ideology that rationalizes turning women into workers. At the same time Rousseau insists that these persons, working at jobs sexlessly, are utterly selfish, concerned only with money and the esteem accorded them, materialistic and vain. They have nothing to respect outside themselves, and their selves are undefinable, just masses of desires. Rousseau describes the bourgeois as a being concerned only with him- or her- or itself, for want of anything else real or compelling to be concerned about (in spite of financing a huge cultural establishment with which the bourgeois tries to persuade himself and others that he has higher concerns), while his self is a product of what others, or "the system," want it to be.

The family, in Rousseau's view, can be defended only if both men and women believe that it is the highest enterprise, more complete and more fulfilling than any career. The belief that being in love is very high and very important is not too difficult to encourage (although easy sex can deflate it). Against the background of love, the vocations tend to pale and appear as at best necessities. In love men and women do care for another, perhaps as much as they care for themselves. This care comes from within; it has a powerful bodily root and is clearly not a product of others' opinions. The difficulty is to extend this passion throughout a lifetime, to keep it singular as it necessarily is at its inception, and to make it culminate in the care of children. This requires education, morality, literature, and reasoning. Persuasion, which is not as powerful as love but in which certain human passions do cooperate— such as love of one's own and longing for immortality—can sometimes convince men and women that raising and educating children is a nobler activity than being a lawyer or a banker, so that those whose family responsibilities exclude them from such professions will not feel that they are maimed by the drudgery of domestic life. These two prerequisites— love of a sexual partner and involvement with children—together can contribute a substantial common good that solicits the individual members of the partnership. This is the only common good of which, according to Rousseau, we know by nature and which is available to us modern men. All other collectivities are the result of force or the contingent private interests of individuals. To put it otherwise, earlier contract teachings provided only a negative motive for abandoning natural individual freedom to enter society—fear of death. Love provides a private motive, and one that does not treat other human beings as means but as ends in themselves. Sex is the only social, or sociable, impulse in man. All other natural impulses leave him isolated, even in the midst of his fellows.

Given the primacy of the family, finally to come to the point, the division of labor between man and woman, their different functions with respect to, and different contributions to, the common good become manifest again. The bodily difference is decisive here. The woman bears the children and nurses them. All the other differences are but corollaries of this first, bodily difference. All that is intolerable to contemporary sensibilities about Rousseau is connected with this point. He asserts that the difference between men and women is natural and that liberation from natural destiny, although surely possible, takes away all gravity from the beings thus liberated. And it is not his fault, Rousseau insists, that nature imposes very special responsibilities on a woman.

In sexual union a woman has two considerations—pleasure and the possibility of pregnancy—whereas a man has only one. Like it or not, the sexual act has far-reaching consequences for her which it does not have for a man. Naturally, without the mediation of law or education, she must make do for herself and for her child. Whatever help she gets comes from the free choice of others, whereas she is constrained by natural necessity. Very simply, it is up to her to constitute the family and hold it together. She must be the one who keeps the man and makes him into a father. Law, once constituted and enforced, can help her, but law will be effective only when it is supported by the inclinations. When men no longer wish to remain with women, they will abandon them and their children. This is still the case even today, when, with the burgeoning divorce rate and enlightenment about men's responsibilities, 90 percent of children remain with their mothers when the parents separate. And this is no accident, as Rousseau sees it, for women have a natural tie to children. They bear them, they nurse them, they are certain they are theirs, and they seem to have an instinctive attachment to children, even to the point of risking their lives for their sake. This is the only natural social bond Rousseau is able to discern. Men will die for their countries or for the women they love, but this sacrifice is not natural or instinctive. It is the product of education and imagination. Naturally men do not have a country and women are not loved in any way other than as means of bodily gratification. At the real foundations, the sole impulse of sociality is that of mother toward child, and all the other seminatural and healthy kinds of sociality cluster around this one. The unit composed of mother and child is the building block out of which society can be constructed. Otherwise only individual self-interest—which means, practically, fear or gain—remains to motivate human beings. The mother's sentiments are the only example we have of unambiguously selfless ones, and these sentiments must be made use of if society is to have an admixture of real concern for others as ends in themselves. In short, women are the link between fathers and children. They are involved with both, and by way of the father's involvement with and faith in the mother, he can become attached to the children, because he loves the mother and because he believes the children are his. Thus the women are the principle of sociality, and it is their responsibility to bring the elements together. Love and motherhood are their domain.

As a result of these reflections Rousseau presents his disagreement with Plato (a disagreement founded on reverence for a great teacher) as one concerning women's modesty. In his total reform of society Socrates begins from an attack on modesty as a mere Greek prejudice. He makes the women in his city strip and exercise naked with the men. Modesty is for Socrates the moving force in the sexual relatedness of men and women, and the removal of the veil it provides takes away the specifically sexual power women have over men. Once this power has been removed, all can look to the city alone as the source of fraternity. The city is de-eroticized in this way. Sexual need can be handled clinically, rationally, in a way most conducive to the utility of the public. Rousseau does not disagree with this analysis. He only argues that the demystification of modesty is not good, that the passionate, erotic relations between male and female are salutary. The understanding of modesty's function is the same for both thinkers. Modesty is both a woman's means of restraining her sexual desire in order to be sure that her children have a father and her means of involving a man with her. Making the assent of her will to his advances important to him is the way sex becomes love, the desire of another's desire. Woman's modesty keeps a man in doubt and makes him believe that he must prove his qualities to her. Modesty is protean. It can be mere coquetry, which forces a man to go through a charade in order to get what he wants, and it can be virtue, yielding only to virtue that is prepared to devote itself to her and to their children. Modesty can inform sexual desire with morality, making it find its satisfaction at least partially in the belief that love is the reward of virtue. It is the source of mystery and romantic illusion in the interplay between the sexes, and the only inner force opposing utilitarianism. In sum, women

[*80*]

by the skillful use of modesty civilize men. That ancient but now unknown custom called courtship was one of the means of enslaving men to women's rule. Men were the ones who willed, but they had to learn to will what women want. In Book V of *Emile* Rousseau presents a little handbook for courtship, outlining the qualities that a man must prove he possesses to his beloved. Only when he has been tested should his suit be accepted by the beloved. She becomes his judge, and he accepts her judgment because he believes that she really wants a good man and knows one when she sees him. His belief in her motivates him to be the kind of man she wants, and Rousseau teaches that this ideal vision of a woman's character is the most potent and natural motive of higher action, one with fewer dangerous consequences than political glory or religious fanaticism, one that has the solid result of procreating the species along with the responsible rearing of children to be good persons and good citizens. A career woman with essentially the same ends as a man could not produce such effects on him, nor would their partnership be more than a business partnership with the ends of each beyond and outside of it. Only if the children are the end can the parents at least in principle be united and the wife in particular avoid being split between her life goals and what she owes to her children.

This interconnectedness of men and women is well illustrated by the theme of male protectiveness. In the *Republic* the class in which the sameness of men and women is instituted consists primarily of warriors. What the same treatment of males and females comes down to in this case is that a man should have no more compunction about sticking a sword through a female than a male in an opposing army and that he should react no differently to the danger or wounds of a female comrade in arms than those of a male. To do so would hamper the rational effectiveness of the soldiers, all just soldiers. Rousseau argues that it is precisely owing to sentiments of social respect for and duty toward women that men become gentle, humane, civil, and responsible to others. The fact that women need protection and men feel they owe it to them is a powerful form of relatedness. Take such sentiments away, by persuading men that they should not feel them or by making women independent, and what takes their place in human relatedness? If the gentlemen on the *Titanic* do not believe that ladies, deserving special consideration, should be the first to leave the ship, then it is every

[*81*]

person for him- or herself. The untrustworthiness of protectiveness, or of men in general, does not constitute a refutation of Rousseau. If men sometimes do behave like gentlemen, it is morally good for them to do so and beneficial to women, particularly if nothing else adequately protects them. It is the mutual dependence of men and women that ties them together. If women do not need men, and men are emotionally and legally able to avoid responsibilities that are always painful and are now made utterly unattractive, men and women will always be psychologically ready for separation and will separate at the first difficulty. A man betrayed and a woman abandoned have always been particularly pitiable, but a world in which neither can happen because neither party really needs or cares for the other would be an abomination of isolation and separateness.

IV

Rousseau's romantic prescriptions may appear to modern eyes to be merely a reaffirmation of age-old sex "roles," but he actually is engaged in a revolutionary reconstitution of the relation between the sexes in the light of the new science of man. Against the background of the abstractness of individual rights, he tries to introduce a sentiment of— not a reasoning about—naturalness which provides real guidance in life. The goodness of nature and its permanence, as opposed to the artificiality of the life created by the conquest of nature with its quest for power after power without being able to generate goals for the attainment of which that power is to be used, is Rousseau's theme, and it has enjoyed an enduring success in back-to-nature and environmentalist movements. It is only the highest expression of that theme, back to the nature of man and woman, which has evoked a negative response in recent times. Rousseau introduced feeling as the counterpoise to calculating reason, which discards such considerations if they do not contribute to economic benefit. In his thought, love of the country tempers conquest of nature, compassion tempers exploitation of men, and eros tempers selfishness or individualism. Recognition and rediscovery of feeling, letting it act as the first principle of action, reconstitutes the world of meaning which modern science and philosophy has dissolved. Thus Rousseau's treatment of love and marriage con-

[82]

centrates not on the rational ordering of the household and the appro-priateness of the partners for their common business but on the inclination of the man and woman for one another. If one reads Plato, Xenophon, Aristotle, or Cicero on marriage, one finds hardly a word about the sexual attraction of the partners. Marriage is for them a civil institution, and the appropriateness of the man and the woman to one another or to the duties of married life has little to do with whether they arouse one another very much physically. Erotic love and marriage are not very good partners, for the former is arbitrary, untamable, unpredict-able, unreasonable, antinomian, and above all unstable. These thinkers talk about duties, not above love. Rousseau, on the other hand, holds that duty can be derived only from prior inclination; the ends of marriage flow from the beginnings in passion. Without such beginnings, there is no substance, no inner vitality in the institution. Love is the root that provides the life to the plant. Without nourishment from it, the plant cannot flourish and grow. The delicate structure of Rousseau's erotic teaching is meant to found the family in all its ramifications without the imposition of alien and alienating law. As the modern state was intended to derive all its force and functions from the primary, natural passion of fear, so Rousseau attempted to found a new kind of family corresponding to and corrective of that state, deriving its force and functions from the sexual passion. Natural freedom comes first; duty is derivative and is assented to in order to exercise the freedom effec-tively. And just as Rousseau's predecessors, Hobbes and Locke, had to remind their readers that, with conventions stripped away, fear and the quest for well-being are natural and powerful, so Rousseau had to remind his readers that sex is natural, attractive, and good. Hobbes and Locke adopted a powerful rhetoric about the unattractive character of the state of nature to reconcile men to the civil state. Rousseau founds a rhetoric about eros to attract men and women to the married state. He is the first philosopher to collaborate with the illusions of love, because they produce a more sublime sense of duty than do the realities of the modern state. This is another perspective on why Rousseau had to write novels. The game of love takes on social and political signif-icance, and men and women must recover their capacity to feel. Nature recaptured gives witness to the sexual attraction of men and women to each other and their mutual differences in possible unity. Sex, far from being sinful, is one of the tiny number of truly natural rights. Actually

ALLAN BLOOM

Rousseau's concentration on the right of following sexual feeling has been adopted by almost everyone, even though his elaboration on its concomitant duties has been rejected.

Rousseau's central reform in the relation between the sexes is an attempt to conciliate nature and freedom by giving women the absolute right to choose their husbands, emancipating them from the authority of their parents. Tocqueville understood this to be the primary fact in the success of American marriage. A woman looks at her suitors and what they offer and freely accepts one or the other or even decides to remain single. This is her way of joining her hopes of sexual gratification and happiness with her responsibility to her children. It is a choice with grave consequences, hence a real choice. Natural necessity weighs on her, but she can inform it with her will and her judgment, and she can test and educate her husband. Thus consent, the only modern principle of legitimacy, is the ground of marriage. It is consent cooperating with natural desire satisfied and controlled by an act of the will. A man, too, must be responsible and willing, but the consequences are so much greater for the woman and her connection with the children so much more inevitable that her choice is the fundamental deed. The man must desire her, perhaps with an idealized and moralized desire, but she must decide about him, no matter how her desire inclines her. She decides whether she can hope to make him care for her and her children, and a large part of this hope is founded on her assurance that she is the moral being who bestows her sexual favors only on the virtuous and who will assuredly make her husband the father of her children. This means that once she has made her choice, it must be absolute or unconditional. She will stick by her promise no matter what, for it is in large measure a promise made to herself and is the source of her self-esteem. Pragmatism can play no role here. She cannot say to herself, "I am a strong and moral being if my partner is; otherwise I follow my lusts," any more than a patriot can say that he will stick by his country as long as it wins. She is the law against which the man's conduct is measured. A woman who has chosen her lot is not just a plaything of authority. She finds dignity in her moral self-esteem even when events disappoint her hopes. All of this applies to a man, too, but to a lesser degree. Woman's morality is the legislative principle of the family and the society of families. There is more possible suffering in her lot but also more nobility. Thus Rousseau makes freedom

[84]

the continuing foundation of the family, and equality in free choice does not require the homogenization of unlike beings. Tocqueville, in his description of the relations between parents and children in America, shows how freedom and equality penetrate the entire family, changing its purposes, the character of the attachments within it, and its structure. Bonds of affection and gratitude take the place of those of authority, tradition, law, and convention. Tocqueville observes that American women have no sympathy with adulteresses, because they, unlike their European counterparts, cannot blame their marriages on unjust external force and hence have no excuse for being defeated by the tension between desire and duty. Equality, rightly understood, makes them moral beings.

And this is the important thing. The issue is not merely marriage but human freedom and morality itself. Sexual conduct is for Rousseau the crucial case proving whether or not human beings can convert natural freedom into moral freedom. Natural freedom means the absence of external impediments, particularly those provided by other human beings, to fulfilling one's desires. But these desires are not freely chosen. They happen to one. And in that sense one is as much a slave to natural lust as are brutes. Only if one can control those desires, not simply by other, more powerful desires but in the name of the good or the ideal, can one make the claim to specifically human dignity, which means autonomy or self-legislation, emancipated from God, nature, or the human law made by others, from heteronomy or alienation. In other words, is man capable of will and hence does he possess human dignity? Rousseau's definition of human freedom is obedience to a law one sets for oneself. With sex he tries to indicate how this is possible or to illustrate the formation of the will.

Autonomous will is, of course, empty. Its content comes from desire. It must choose to satisfy desire or deny it satisfaction. If one is to prove that it is really will, it must not be determined by anything other than the good itself. It must be able to motivate forgoing of satisfaction or happiness in the name of the good. But what is the good if it is not the satisfaction of desire? Sex provides the best case for seeing and solving the problem. Sex is simply natural lust. But out of it comes the need to live with other human beings and to make agreements with them. Sex, unlike hunger, generates ideal fantasies of virtue and fidelity. One can imagine what one and one's partner must be in order

[*85*]

to satisfy and not do harm to one another. If one can be motivated by that ideal to control the sexuality out of which it comes, then one can be said to be exercising a control over oneself that is produced by oneself, to be living one's own ideal. The tension between duty and desire is imposed not from without by society but from within by desire, deriving the ideal from itself with the aid of a union of reason and feeling. This is a substantial account of the famous generalization or universalization of desire which constitutes morality. The promise made in marriage, which both parties presumably second with their sexual desire, must be able to survive the change in that desire. Otherwise the promise is nothing but animal sexual desire masquerading as morality in order to fulfill its end. Rousseau finds that sex is the only one of the natural desires that might possibly produce this conversion—truly pointed toward another, powerful, and capable of producing sublime objects. Experience of the heroism of lovers distinguishes sex from hunger as an ideal force. This is the natural way to love another as oneself.

Love is Rousseau's solution to the problem of establishing a non-mercenary morality within the context of rational liberalism. From this first obligation flow all the others—to children, to the civil society that protects the family. Modern regimes understand themselves to be founded by a contract. The contract as presented by its teachers is purely negative, joined in because, without the state's power, the life of natural freedom is too precarious. This is an unsociable sociability and one not sufficient to make the social contract sacred or to justify the sacrifice of life to it. No other contract carries with it the requirement that one die in fulfilling it. Naturally only the marriage contract is positive, made not only for the individual benefit of those who enter into it, and is felt to demand, in case of need, the supreme sacrifice. Rousseau makes the sexual contract into the essence of the social contract in order to provide society with a positive impulse. Marriage is the contract of contracts, and, if this one can be fulfilled in good faith, so can the others that can be made to be derivative from it. A family man can be said to be moral for good reason as an individual cannot, and marriage is something almost all men and women must face. It does not have the abstract character of modern politics, where moral obligation has no real contact with everyday life and concerns people one has never met. The pleasures and duties of marriage are truly lived.

[86]

The discussion of all this moved from the texts of moralists into its more proper place in nineteenth-century novels, so much of whose inspiration was provided by Rousseau. They were the true educators of the democratic taste, appealing to the imaginative and sensitive faculties that apprehend such truths. The interplay between man and woman and the effort to show forth their respective natures as they relate to one another were invested with a new seriousness. The fairest artistic genius dedicated itself to discerning and depicting the mode of being of men and women together; no more subtle, delicate, or profound elaboration of this theme can be imagined. Current moral indignation deprives us of this fertile source of insight into human nature. In it the true interest of life was the romantic, in the discovery of inclinations that lead to suitable marriage, as in Jane Austen, in stories about young men whose great passion for a woman reveals the dreariness of ambition in bourgeois social and political life, as in Stendhal. But above all and everywhere, adultery was the great theme. Not primarily because it was forbidden, shocking, and titillating for readers, although it was all of them. Adultery was the necessary question because it represented *the* test of human moral capacity, of the deepest commitment, of the wholeness or unity of man in the relation of his bodily pleasures to his tenderest and noblest spirituality, of the possible triumph of duty over desire. Marital fidelity after Rousseau was the core of the moral problem, the sacred, the social bond. The meaning of adultery, committing it or resisting it, is of the greatest interest to those who have put their eggs in the marital basket. Adultery in the romantic world is the equivalent of betrayal of one's country in the political world (the cases of Coriolanus and Alcibiades, for example). The artist allows the readers to apprehend the stakes in great choices. Adultery really concerned the metaphysical issue of human freedom and responsibility. This conviction is what animated the best novelists—Tolstoy in *Anna Karenina*, for instance—and gives gravity to works on themes that were formerly despised. When adultery lost its cosmic significance, novels about love lost theirs. The connection between aesthetics and morals, on which Rousseau and Kant so insisted, is nowhere else so clear.

To conclude on this question, Rousseau saw something miraculous in sex. Body can become spirit. Seminal effervescence becomes creativity in animating the imagination. He was among the earliest thinkers, if he was not himself the earliest, to see in this creativity, as opposed to reason, the specific difference of man. The beautiful object that solicits desire and leads it upward is the creation of man the artist. This beautiful ideal forms in turn a model of behavior with respect to itself which is the final cause of noble behavior. The work of art both imitates and encourages such behavior. The beautiful and the moral are inseparable. Rousseauan morals, aesthetics, and psychology are the grandest description of the sublime and sublimation in an egalitarian society that needs both while threatening both. We need him, if only for fear that we forget the very question.

[4]

Equality of Opportunity
and Liberal Theory

WILLIAM GALSTON

I

Every society embodies a conception of justice. The modern liberal society is no exception. Two principles are of particular importance. First, goods and services that fall within the sphere of basic needs are to be distributed on the basis of need, and the needs of all individuals are to be regarded as equally important. Second, many opportunities outside the sphere of need are to be allocated to individuals through a competition in which all have a fair chance to participate.[1]

The latter principle entered American political thought under the rubric of "equality of opportunity." Much of American social history can be interpreted as a struggle between those who wished to widen the scope of its application and those who sought to restrict it. Typically, its proponents have promoted *formal* equality of opportunity by attacking religious, racial, sexual, and other barriers to open competition among individuals. And they have promoted *substantive* equality of opportunity by broadening access to the institutions that develop socially valued talents.

1. William Galston, "Moral Personality and Liberal Theory: John Rawls's 'Dewey Lectures,' " *Political Theory* 10 (1982): 514–16.

Recently, equality of opportunity has come under renewed attack. Conservatives charge that it fosters excessive public intervention in essentially private or voluntary relations. Radicals point with scorn to the competitive selfishness it fosters and to the unequal outcomes it permits. In the face of such assaults, liberals seem bewildered and defensive.

In this paper I want to sketch the grounds on which I believe equality of opportunity can be defended, and on that basis reply to the strictures of its critics. In the course of doing so I shall revise the generally accepted understanding of this principle in several respects. As I interpret it, equality of opportunity is less juridical and more teleological than is commonly supposed. It rests on an understanding of human equality more substantive than "equality of concern and respect."[2] It is broader than the traditional concept of meritocracy. And it is embedded in a larger vision of a good society.

My argument proceeds in four steps. First, I shall examine in summary fashion some propositions that provide the philosophical foundation for equality of opportunity. Next I shall explore the strengths and limits of four kinds of arguments commonly offered in defense of this principle. Third, I shall discuss some difficulties that attend the translation of the abstract principle into concrete social practices. Finally, I shall briefly respond to three recent critics of equality of opportunity.

II

Let me begin my foundational argument with two propositions about individuals. Proposition 1: *All judgments concerning justice and injustice are ultimately relative to individuals* who are benefited or harmed, honored or dishonored in the distribution of contested goods. When we say that a group has been treated unjustly, we mean that the individuals comprising that group have been so treated. It would make no sense to say that every member of a group has been treated justly but that nevertheless the group has been treated unjustly. Membership in

2. Ronald Dworkin, *Taking Rights Seriously* (Cambridge: Harvard University Press, 1978), pp. 272–73.

the group does not constitute an additional basis of entitlement beyond individual circumstances.

The insistence on the individual as the benchmark of justice is essential to the principle of equality of opportunity and to liberal theory as a whole. Not surprisingly, this premise has been sharply questioned. Communitarian critics of liberalism contend that the physical boundaries of individuals do not correspond to the social unities from which we ought to take our bearings. We become human only in society, they argue. Our language, our customs, our ambitions—everything that defines us is formed in social interchange. To be human is to participate in activities that are essentially social and relational. We are inextricably fused with others through that participation. It is impossible to say "I" without meaning "we."[3]

This argument is, I believe, a non sequitur. While the formative power of society is surely decisive, it is nevertheless *individuals* that are being shaped. I may share everything with others. But it is *I* that shares them—an independent consciousness, a separate locus of pleasure and pain, a demarcated being with interests to be advanced or suppressed. My interpretation of my own good may be socially determined, but it is still *my* good, and it may well not be fully congruent with the good of others. Thus, as we counter the hyperindividualism of those who deny the existence of any social bonds with or moral obligations to others, it is important not to fall into the hyperorganicism that denies the ineradicable separateness of our individual existences.[4]

I turn now to my second proposition: *All principles of justice— including liberal principles—rest on some view of the good life for individuals*. It is now widely believed that principles of justice need not rest on this foundation, and that liberalism is precisely the theory that rests on the studied refusal to specify the human good. This is the premise underlying John Rawls's so-called priority of the right over the good, as well as the neutrality thesis of Ronald Dworkin and Bruce Ackerman.[5] But it is mistaken. Let me cite just one reason why.

3. For the most sophisticated presentation of this thesis, see Michael Sandel, *Liberalism and the Limits of Justice* (Cambridge: Cambridge University Press, 1982).
4. For the best example of what I call "hyperindividualism," see Robert Nozick, *Anarchy, State, and Utopia* (New York: Basic Books, 1974), pp. 30–33.
5. John Rawls, *A Theory of Justice* (Cambridge: Belknap Press of Harvard University Press, 1971); Ronald Dworkin, "Liberalism," in Stuart Hampshire, ed., *Public*

Every principle of justice is intended to guide human conduct. Confronted with such a principle, the skeptic is entitled to ask, "Why should I be just?" It certainly won't do to reply, "Be just because the moral point of view requires it." A well-formed answer, I suggest, must link justice to intelligible motives for action. That is, it must invoke some conception of the good as the end of action—happiness, perfection, moral freedom, or the like. Even the strong claim that justice is a requirement of reason derives its hortatory force from the assumed goodness of the rational life.[6]

Some views of the human good argue for a summum bonum—one best way of life on the basis of which all others can be judged and rank-ordered. It may well be possible to defend such a view. For my present purposes, however, a more latitudinarian approach will suffice, along the following lines.

Every human being is born with a wide range of potential talents. Some ought not to be encouraged—a capacity for ingenious and guiltless cruelty, for example. Among the capacities of an individual that are in some sense worth developing, a small subset are comprehensive enough to serve as organizing principles for an entire life. The fullest possible development of one or more of these capacities is an important element of the good life for that individual.

Experience teaches us that individuals vary widely. Each of us is naturally gifted along some dimensions and inept along others. Some are naturally good at many things, others at few. Experience also suggests that talents vary qualitatively. Some are common and rudimentary, others are rare and highly prized.

Here I want to propose a notion of human equality that is essential to equality of opportunity as I understand it. I want to suggest that in spite of profound differences among individuals, the full development of each individual—however great or limited his or her natural capacities—is equal in moral weight to that of every other. For any individuals A and B, a policy that leads to the full development of A and partial

---

and Private Morality (Cambridge: Cambridge University Press, 1978); Bruce Ackerman, Social Justice in the Liberal State (New Haven: Yale University Press, 1980).

6. For a fuller discussion, see William Galston, Justice and the Human Good (Chicago: University of Chicago Press, 1980), pp. 55–56, 279–80, and "Defending Liberalism," American Political Science Review 76 (1982): 621–29.

development of *B* is, *ceteris paribus*, equal in value to a policy that fully develops *B* while restricting *A*'s development to the same degree. Thus a policy that neglects the educable retarded so that they do not learn how to care for themselves and must be institutionalized is, considered in itself, as bad as one that reduces extraordinary gifts to mere normality.

On one level, this proposal runs counter to our moral intuitions. It seems hard to deny that the full realization of high capacities is preferable to the full development of lower, more limited capacities. But this consideration is not decisive.

We would of course prefer a world in which everyone's innate capacities were more extensive than they are at present, and we would choose to be (say) mathematically talented rather than congenitally retarded. Accordingly, we would prefer *for ourselves* the full development of more extensive capacities to the full development of lesser ones. But it does not follow that whenever the developmental interests of different individuals come into conflict, the development of higher or more extensive capacities is to be given priority. A policy that focuses exclusively on the intrinsic worth of our capacities treats the characteristics of separate individuals as an artificial, disembodied unity, ignoring the fact that they have no existence apart from the individuals in whom they inhere.

It may be argued, nonetheless, that there is something more horrible about the incomplete development of great capacities than about the waste of lesser gifts. Perhaps so. But one might say with equal justice that it is more horrible for someone who can be taught to speak to be condemned to a life of inarticulate quasi-animality than it is for someone who could have been a great mathematician to lead an ordinary life. Our intuitions about the relative desirability of the best cases are more or less counterbalanced by the relative unacceptability of the worst.[7]

I can now offer a partial definition of a good society. In such a society, the range of social possibilities will equal the range of human possibilities. Each worthy capacity, that is, will find a place within it. No one will be compelled to flee elsewhere in search of opportunities for development, the way ambitious young people had to flee farms

7. Galston, *Justice and the Human Good*, pp. 159–62.

and small towns in nineteenth-century societies. Further, each worthy capacity will be treated fairly in the allocation of resources available for individual development within that society.

These criteria, I suggest, are more fully satisfied in a liberal society than in any other. Historically, liberal societies have come closer than any others to achieving the universality that excludes no talent or virtue. The development of great gifts encounters few material or political impediments. The development of ordinary gifts is spurred by education and training open to all. Warriors, statesmen, poets, philosophers, men and women of devoted piety—all are welcomed and accommodated. The fundamental argument for a diverse society is not—as some believe—that our reason is incompetent to judge among possible ways of life. It is rather that the human good is not one thing but many things.

Although the principle of equality of opportunity is embedded in this kind of society, it is nonetheless commonly thought to presuppose a sharp distinction between the natural endowments of individuals and their social environment. The life chances of individuals, it is argued, should not be determined by such factors as race, economic class, and family background. To the extent that these factors do tend to affect the development and exercise of individual talents, it is the task of social policy to alleviate their force. If malnutrition stunts mental and physical development, then poor children must be fed by the community. If social deprivation leaves some children irreparably behind before they start first grade, then compensatory preschool programs are essential.

The proposition that natural but not social differences should affect individual life chances raises a number of difficult problems. To begin with, natural differences are usually viewed as genetic endowments not subject to external intervention. But increasingly, natural endowments are malleable, and the time may not be far off when they can be more predictably altered than can social circumstances. This eventuality will transform not only the distinction between the natural and the social but also its normative consequences. To that extent that, for example, modern techniques can overcome genetic defects or even determine genetic endowments, disputes will arise among families over access to these scarce and expensive techniques. Before the opportunity to develop one's capacities will come the opportunity to have certain capacities to develop. At this point—as Bernard Williams rightly suggests— equality of opportunity will merge into broader issues of absolute equality and the morality of genetic intervention.[8]

Assuming that we are still some time away from the obliteration of the naturally given, we can still ask why differences of social background are thought to be impermissible determinants of social outcomes and, conversely, why natural differences are thought to be appropriate determinants.

Why shouldn't the chief's eldest child be the next chief? This question is seldom asked because it seems absurd to us. We take it for granted that a competitive system ought to winnow out the candidate "best qualified" and that family membership is utterly irrelevant to this selection. But of course it need not be. If the tribe is held together by shared loyalty based in part on family sentiments, the chief's child may be uniquely qualified. Descent may be an important ingredient of social legitimacy and therefore an important claim to rule, especially when other sources of legitimacy have been weakened. Contemporary Lebanon, where sons gain power from fathers and assume their murdered brothers' burdens, typifies this sort of society.

Underlying the usual distinction between social and natural differences is the moral intuition that social outcomes should be determined by factors over which individuals have control. But the wealth and social standing of one's family are facts over which individuals cannot exercise control, and therefore they shouldn't matter.

The difficulty with this argument is that individuals don't control their natural endowments any more than they do their ancestry. The requirement that the basis on which we make claims must somehow be generated through our own efforts amounts to a nullification of the very procedure of claiming *anything*.[9]

The costs of this conclusion are very high. Every conception of justice presupposes the distinction between valid and invalid claims, which in turn rests on some facts about individuals. There can be no theory of justice without some notion of individual desert, and no notion of

8. Bernard Williams, "The Idea of Equality," in Peter Laslett and W. G. Runciman, eds., *Philosophy, Politics, and Society*, 2d ser. (Oxford: Basil Blackwell, 1962), pp. 110–31.

9. Michael Zuckert, "Justice Deserted: A Critique of Rawls' *A Theory of Justice*," *Polity* 13 (1981): 477; Nozick, *Anarchy, State, and Utopia*, pp. 224–27.

individual desert that doesn't eventually come to rest on some "undeserved" characteristics of individuals.

Some may wish to conclude that the cause of justice is lost. I disagree, because I reject the premise of the preceding argument. The world's fastest sprinter doesn't "deserve" his natural endowment of speed, but surely he deserves to win the race established to measure and honor this excellence. There is nothing in principle wrong with a conception of individual desert that rests on the possession of natural gifts.

I would conclude, rather, that the normative distinction between social facts and natural endowments is not so sharp as most interpretations of equality of opportunity presuppose. This distinction provided the historical impetus for the development of the principle: the triumph of meritocratic over patriarchal and hereditary norms is an oft-told tale. But philosophically, the social/natural distinction must be reinterpreted as the distinction between relevant and irrelevant reasons for treating individuals in certain manners.

To further this reinterpretation, I want to examine four ways in which equality of opportunity can be defended.

III

First—and most obviously—equality of opportunity can be justified as a principle of *efficiency*. Whatever the goals of a community may be, they are most likely to be achieved when the individuals most capable of performing the tasks that promote those goals are allowed to do so. Such efficiency, it may be argued, requires a system that allows individuals to declare their candidacy for positions they prefer and then selects the ablest. From this standpoint, equality of opportunity is a dictate of instrumental rationality, a measure of collective devotion to social goals.

But a complication crops up immediately. Competition among individuals to fill social roles may not produce aggregate efficiency, even if the most talented is chosen to fill each individual role.

To see why, consider a two-person society with two tasks. Suppose that person *A* can perform both tasks better than person *B* and is by an absolute measure better at the first task than at the second. If *A* is only slightly better than *B* at the first but much better at the second, it is more productive for the society as a whole to allocate the first task to *B*, even though *A* will then not be doing what he does best.

In actual societies, the differential rewards attached to tasks can produce comparable distortions. If (say) lawyers are paid much more than teachers, the talent pool from which lawyers are selected is likely to be better stocked. Teachers will then tend to be mediocre, even if the best are selected from among the candidates who present themselves. This circumstance may well impose aggregate costs on society, at least in the long run.

These difficulties arise for two reasons. First, applying equality of opportunity to a society characterized by division of labor produces a set of individual competitions whose aggregate results will fall short of the best that society could achieve through more centralized coordination among these contests. Second, equality of opportunity embodies an element of individual liberty. Individuals can choose neither the rules of various competitions nor their outcomes. But they can choose which game to play. The fact that society as a whole will benefit if I perform a certain task does not mean that I can be coerced to perform it. Within limits, I can choose which talents to develop and exercise, and I can refuse to enter specific competitions, even if I would surely emerge victorious. "From each according to his ability" is not the principle of a liberal society, for the simple reason that the individual is regarded as the owner of his or her capacities. Equality of opportunity is a meritocratic principle, but it is applied to competitions among self-selected individuals.

I do not wish to suggest that this liberty is anything like absolute. Duties to other individuals, particularly family members who have made sacrifices on my behalf, may require me to develop and exercise certain abilities. Similarly, duties to my country may require me to become a first-rate general or physicist, if I am capable of doing so. But after all such duties are taken into account, there will still be a range of choice into which a liberal society should not intrude. This will always be a barrier to the single-minded pursuit of efficiency, and to the use of coercive meritocracy to achieve it.

The second justification of equality of opportunity focuses on the notion of *desert*. For each social position, it is argued, a certain range of personal qualities may be considered relevant. Individuals who possess these qualities to an outstanding degree deserve those positions.

A fair competition guided by equality of opportunity will allow exemplary individuals to be identified and rewarded.

Many critics have objected to this line of reasoning. It is a mistake, they argue, to regard social positions as prizes. In athletic competition, first prize goes to the one who has performed best. It would be inappropriate to take future performance into account or to regard present performance in the context of future possibilities. The award of the prize looks only backward to what has already happened. The prize winner has established desert through completed performance. In the case of social positions, on the other hand, the past is of interest primarily as an index of future performance. The alleged criterion of desert is thus reducible to considerations of efficiency.

This critique contains elements of truth, but I believe that the sharp contrast it suggests is overdrawn. After all, societies do not just declare the existence of certain tasks to be performed. They also make known, at least in general terms, the kinds of abilities that will count as qualifications to perform these tasks. Relying on this shared public understanding, young people strive to acquire and display these abilities. If they succeed in doing so, they have earned the right to occupy the corresponding positions. They deserve them. It would therefore be wrong to breach these legitimate expectations, just as it would be wrong to tell the victorious runner, "Sorry. We know you crossed the finish line first, but we've decided to give the prize to the runner who stopped to help a fallen teammate."

To be sure, circumstances may prevent society from honoring legitimate desert claims. Individuals may spend years preparing themselves for certain occupations, only to find that economic or demographic changes have rendered their skills outmoded. Socially established expectations cannot be risk-free—a fact that security-seeking young people are not always quick to grasp. But this fact does not distinguish social competition from athletic competition. The Americans who worked so hard for the 1980 Olympic Games, only to be denied the right to compete, were deeply disappointed, but they could not maintain that they had been treated unjustly.

In short, no clear line can be drawn between tasks and prizes. Many tasks *are* prizes—opportunities to perform activities that are intrinsically or socially valuable. These prizes are of a special character—forward-looking rather than complete in themselves—and this gives rise to legitimate disagreement about the criteria that should govern their distribution. There is no science that permits completely reliable inferences from past to future performance in any occupation. But once criteria, however flawed, have been laid down, they create a context within which claims of desert can be established and must be honored if possible. Performance criteria may be altered, but only after existing claims have been discharged, and only in a manner that gives all individuals the fairest possible chance to redirect their efforts.

A third kind of justification of equality of opportunity focuses on *personal development*. When a society devotes resources to education and training, when it encourages individuals to believe that their life chances will be significantly related to their accomplishments, and when it provides an attractive array of choices, there is good reason to believe that individuals will be moved to develop some portion of their innate capacities. Thus, it may be argued, equality of opportunity is the principle of task allocation most conducive to a crucial element of the human good.

I accept this argument. But it has significant limitations. It ignores, for example, ways in which individuals may benefit from performing certain tasks even if they are less competent to do so than others. If an apprentice is not permitted to perform the activities of his craft, he cannot increase his competence. In this process, the master craftsman must be willing to accept errors and inefficiencies. This is true even if the learner can never achieve the full competence of the best practitioner. Even individuals of mediocre talents can increase their knowledge, skill, and self-confidence when they are allowed to discharge demanding responsibilities. Thus developmental considerations may suggest rotating some tasks fairly widely rather than restricting them to the most able.

In addition, most individuals can achieve excellence in specific demanding tasks only when they concentrate on mastering that task to the exclusion of all others. Equality of opportunity is thus linked to the division of labor, to specialization, and to the principle of "one person, one job." An argument of considerable antiquity questions the human consequences of this principle. Perhaps it is better for individuals to be minimally competent and developed in many areas rather than al-

[99]

lowing most of their capacities to lie fallow. Perhaps a system of task assignment that deemphasized competence in favor of variety would be preferable.

These considerations raise a broader issue. Human activities have both external and internal dimensions. On the one hand, they effect changes in the natural world and in the lives of others. On the other hand, they alter—develop, stunt, pervert—the character and talent of those who perform them. Neither dimension can be given pride of place; neither can be ignored.

Without a measure of physical security and material well-being, no society can afford to devote resources to individual development or to exempt individuals from material production for any portion of their lives. In societies living at the margin, child labor is a necessity and scholarly leisure is an unaffordable luxury. But structuring a social and economic system to promote productive efficiency is justified only by physical needs and by the material preconditions of development itself. Thus a fundamental perversion occurs when the subordination of development to production continues beyond that point. A wealthy community that determines the worth of all activities by the extent to which they add to its wealth has forgotten what wealth is for. A system of training, education, and culture wholly subservient to the system of production denies the fuller humanity of its participants.[10]

For these reasons, I suggest, a prosperous society must carefully consider not only how it allocates its tasks but also how it defines and organizes the tasks it allocates. The very concern for individual development that makes equality of opportunity so attractive leads beyond that principle to basic questions of social structure.

Finally, equality of opportunity may be defended on the grounds that it is conducive to *personal satisfaction*. Within the limits of competence, individuals are permitted to choose their lives' central activity, and they are likely to spend much of their time in occupations they are competent to perform. No system can guarantee satisfaction, of course. But one that reduces to a minimum the compulsory elements of labor and allows individuals to feel competent in the course of their labor will come closer than any alternative.

While this argument is probably correct, it is important to keep its

10. Galston, *Justice and the Human Good*, pp. 261–62.

limits in mind. To begin with, the satisfaction derived from an activity is not always proportional to our ability to perform it. We may want to do what we cannot do very well, and we may obtain more pleasure from doing what we regard as a higher task in a mediocre manner than from doing a lower task very well. In addition, in a system fully governed by equality of opportunity, there would be no external causes of failure and no alternative to self-reproach for the inability to achieve personal ambitions.

An equal opportunity system stimulates many to strive for what they cannot attain. By broadening horizons, it may well increase frustration. Of course, this is not necessarily a bad thing. Such a system does induce many who can excel to develop themselves more fully. It is not clear that a system that increases both achievement and frustration is inferior to one that increases the subjective satisfaction of the less talented only by decreasing the motivation of the more talented to realize their abilities. And many people not capable of the highest accomplishments will nevertheless develop and achieve more in a context that infuses them with a desire to excel. A permanent gap between what we are and what we want to be need not be debilitating. On the contrary, it can be a barrier to complacency, a source of modesty, an incentive for self-discipline, and a ground of genuine respect for excellence.

IV

I remarked at the outset that the principle of equality of opportunity gains both content and justification from the society in which it is embedded. There are, I believe, four major dimensions along which this abstract principle is rendered socially concrete: first, the range of possibilities available within a society; second, the manner in which these activities are delimited and organized; third, the criteria governing the assignment of individuals to particular activities; and finally, the manner in which activities are connected to external goods such as money, power, and status.

I need not add much to the previous discussion of possibilities. A good society is maximally inclusive, allowing the greatest possible scope for the development and exercise of worthy talents.

Opportunities for development are affected not just by the kinds of activities that take place within a society but also by their manner of organization. Consider the provision of health care. At present in the United States, doctors, nurses, orderlies, and administrators perform specific ranges of activities, linked to one another by rigid lines of authority. It is possible—and probably desirable—to redraw these boundaries of specialization. Nurses, for example, could well be given more responsibility for tasks now performed by doctors, particularly in areas where judgment, experience, and sensitivity to the needs of specific individuals are more significant than are high levels of technical training. Similarly, it is possible to reorganize the process of production. At some plants, small groups of workers collectively produce entire automobiles, performing the required operations sequentially in the group's own area rather than along an assembly line. Proposals to expand managerial decision making to include production workers have been tried out in a number of European countries.

Behind all such suggestions lies the belief that the existing organization of social tasks rests more on habit and special privilege than on an impartial analysis of social or individual benefit. Occupational hierarchies in which all creativity and authority are confined to a few tasks while all the rest enforce routine drudgery are typically justified on the grounds of efficiency. Maintaining a certain quality and quantity of goods and services is said to demand this kind of hierarchy. In general, there is little evidence to support this proposition and much to question it. Besides, as we have seen, there are other things to consider—in particular, the effect of tasks on the development and satisfaction of the individuals who perform them. Equal opportunity requires an appropriate balance between the preconditions of productive efficiency and the internal consequences of tasks—a balance that may well depend on a far-reaching reorganization of social tasks.

Let me assume that a society has actually reached agreement on such a balance. The assignment of individuals to the tasks embodied in that agreement will remain controversial, because criteria of assignment are open to reasonable dispute. Some considerations are clearly irrelevant. Barring aberrant background circumstances, such factors as the color of one's hair or eyes should have no bearing on one's chances of becoming a doctor, because they have no bearing on one's capacity to practice the medical art. But beyond such obvious cases, there is disagreement about the nature of the good doctor. In the prevailing view the good doctor is one who is capable of mastering a wide variety of techniques and employing them appropriately. But dissenters suggest that moral criteria should be given equal weight: the good doctor cares more about her patients' welfare than about her own material advancement, gives great weight to need in distributing her services, never loses sight of the humanity of her patients. Still others believe that the willingness to practice where medical needs are greatest is crucial. They urge that great weight be given to the likelihood—or the promise— that a prospective doctor will provide health care to rural areas, small towns, urban ghettos, or other localities lacking adequate care. From this standpoint, otherwise dubious criteria such as geographical origin or even race might become very important.

This dispute cannot be resolved in the abstract. The relative weight accorded the technical, moral, and personal dimensions will vary with the needs and circumstances of particular societies. It will also vary among specialties within professions. In the selection of brain surgeons, technical mastery is probably paramount. For pediatricians, human understanding is far more important. Whatever the criteria, they must be made as explicit as possible, so that individuals can make informed commitments to courses of training and preparation. Those who control the selection are not free to vary publicly declared criteria once they have engendered legitimate expectations.

I turn now to the connection between activities and external goods. Here my point is simple. A fair competition may demonstrate my qualification for a particular occupation. But the talents that so qualify me do not entitle me to whatever external rewards happen to be attached to that occupation. I may nevertheless be entitled to them, but an independent line of argument is needed to establish that fact. So, for example, in accordance with public criteria, my technical competence may entitle me to a position as a brain surgeon. It does not follow that I am entitled to half a million dollars a year. Even if we grant what is patently counterfactual in the case of doctors—that compensation is determined by the market—the principle of task assignment in accordance with talents does not commit us to respect market outcomes. Indeed, the kind of competition inherent in a system of equal opportunity bears no clear relation to the competition characteristic of the market.

This distinction has an important consequence. Many thinkers oppose meritocratic systems on the ground that there is no reason why differences of talent should generate or legitimate vast differences in material rewards. They are quite right. But this is not an objection to meritocracy as such. It is an objection to the way society assigns *rewards* to tasks, not to the way it assigns *individuals* to tasks.

Indeed, one could argue that current salary inequalities should be reversed. Most highly paid jobs in our society are regarded as intrinsically desirable by the people who perform them. In moments of candor, most business executives, doctors, lawyers, generals, and college professors admit that they would want to continue in their professions even at considerably lower income levels. The incomes generally associated with such occupations cannot then be justified as socially necessary incentives.

There are, however, some rewards that are intrinsically related to tasks themselves. The most obvious is the gratification obtained from performing them. Another is status. Although I cannot prove it, it seems likely that there is a hierarchy of respect and prestige independent of income, correlated with what is regarded as the intrinsic worth of activities. Tasks involving extraordinary traits of mind and character or the ability to direct the activities of others are widely prized.

Finally, certain activities may entail legitimate claims to some measure of power and authority. As Aristotle pointed out, there are inherent hierarchical relations among specialized functions. The architect guides the work of the bricklayer and the plasterer. Moreover, if members of a community have agreed on a goal, knowledge that conduces to the achievement of that goal provides a rational basis for authority. If everyone wishes to cross the ocean and arrive at a common destination, then the skilled navigator has a rational claim to the right to give orders. But the navigator's proper authority is limited in both extent and time. It does not regulate the community's nonnavigational activities, and it vanishes when all reach their destination.

V

At the outset of this paper I said that I would employ my analysis of equality of opportunity to reply to its critics, radical and conservative. I wish, in conclusion, to touch on three arguments that are frequently brought against equality of opportunity.

[*104*]

The first objection is the *libertarian*, raised in its purest form by Robert Nozick. According to Nozick, equality of opportunity understates the individualistic character of human existence. Life is not a race with a starting line, a finish line, a clearly designated judge, and a complex of attributes to be measured. Rather, there are only individuals, agreeing to give to and receive from each another.[11]

I believe that this contention overlooks important social facts. Within every community, certain kinds of abilities are generally prized. Being excluded from an equal chance to develop them means that one is unlikely to have much of value to exchange with others: consider the problem of hard-core unemployment when the demand for unskilled labor is declining. To be sure, there is more than one social contest, but the number is limited. In a society in which rising educational credentials are demanded even for routine tasks, exclusion from the competition for education and training—or inclusion on terms that amount to a handicap—will make it very difficult to enter the system of exchange. Equality of opportunity acknowledges these prerequisites to full participation in social competition, and it therefore legitimates at least some of the social interventions needed to permit full participation.

The second objection is the *communitarian*. According to this view, advanced by John Schaar among others, even the most perfect competition is insufficient, because competition is a defective mode of existence. It sets human beings apart from each other and pits them against one another, in an essentially destructive struggle.[12]

Certainly an equal opportunity system contains some competitive elements. But not all forms of competition are bad. Some competition brings human beings closer together, into communities of shared endeavor and mutual respect. Consider the embrace of two exhausted boxers at the end of a match, or even the spontaneous bond between Anwar Sadat and Golda Meir at their first face-to-face encounter. Moreover, competition can be mutually beneficial. Scientific competition may produce simultaneous discoveries, neither of which would have occurred without the presence of the competitor; gymnastic competition may inspire two perfect performances. And finally, the traditional antithesis between competition and community is too simple. Community

11. Nozick, *Anarchy, State, and Utopia*, pp. 235–38.
12. John Schaar, "Equality of Opportunity, and Beyond," in J. Roland Pennock and John W. Chapman, eds., *Nomos 9: Equality* (New York: Atherton, 1967).

rests on some agreement. A competitive system can be a form of community if most participants are willing to accept the principle of competition.

The third objection to equality of opportunity is the *democratic*. According to this objection—articulated by Michael Walzer, among others—equality of opportunity is at best a limited principle because it cannot apply to the sphere of politics. Technical expertise may confer a limited authority. But because there is no rationally binding conception of the good, there is no technique for selecting the ends of political life. Political power does not look *up* to Platonic ideas, but rather *around* to prevailing opinions: "The proper exercise of power is nothing more than the direction of the city in accordance with the civic consciousness or public spirit of the citizens."[13]

I do not believe that any contemporary political thinker has adequately defended the crucial premise of this argument: that no rational theory of political ends is available. But let me set this question to one side and focus briefly on what it means to direct a community in accordance with its own self-understanding.

At one juncture Walzer notes that a majority of citizens "might well misunderstand the logic of their own institutions or fail to apply consistently the principles they professed to hold."[14] There may, then, be a kind of expertise in the understanding of civic consciousness that cuts against simply majoritarian institutions and democratic procedures. In *Brown* v. *Board of Education*, for example, the U.S. Supreme Court rendered a decision that would certainly have been rejected by majority vote at the time, but that was ultimately accepted as the authoritative interpretation of American principles.

More broadly: I would argue there are distinctive political excellences and virtues; they are necessary for the success of all political orders, including democracies; and they do constitute one claim—though not the only claim—to political authority, because they contribute to needed cooperation and to the achievement of shared purposes. Without them, a political community will lose its bearings and its self-confidence. It would be very fortunate if these virtues were widely distributed. But experience suggests that the percentage of individuals who possess them to any significant degree within a given community will be small.

13. Michael Walzer, *Spheres of Justice: A Defense of Pluralism and Equality* (New York: Basic Books, 1983), p. 287.
14. Ibid., p. 99.

This does not necessarily mean that democracy is based on a mistake. As Jefferson saw, the problem of democracy is to achieve some convergence of participation, consent, and excellence. He believed that this problem is soluble—in part through social and political institutions that single out the natural *aristoi*, develop their special gifts, and reliably promote them to high office. From this standpoint, the purpose of elections is not just to register opinion but also to identify excellence. Indeed, the test of an electoral system is its propensity to confer the mantle of leadership on those most worthy to lead. Properly understood, the distribution of power in democracies is not wholly distinct from, but rather partly governed by, the merit-based principle of equal opportunity.

[5]

Self-Ownership, World-Ownership,
and Equality

G. A. COHEN

The first man who, having enclosed a piece of land, took it
into his head to say, "This is mine," and found people simple
enough to believe him, was the true founder of civil society.
The human race would have been spared endless crimes, wars,
murders, and horrors if someone had pulled up the stakes or
filled in the ditch and cried out to his fellow men, "Do not
listen to this impostor! You are lost if you forget that the fruits
of the earth belong to everyone, and the earth to no one!"

—Jean-Jacques Rousseau,
Discourse on Inequality

. . . the original "appropriation" of opportunities by private
owners involves investment in exploration, in detailed inves-
tigation and appraisal by trial and error of the findings, in
development work of many kinds necessary to secure and
market a product—besides the cost of buying off or killing or
driving off previous claimants.

—Frank H. Knight, "Some Fallacies
in the Interpretation of Social Cost"

I thank Simon Courtenay, Hillel Steiner, Steven Walt, Erik Wright, and Arnold
Zuboff for their criticisms of a draft of this paper.

I. Introduction

1. In Part I of this paper I describe the range and motivation of a research project on which I am currently engaged. In Part II I offer a relatively finished version of its first installment.

The themes of the project are suggested by the title of the paper. I embarked on the project in an attempt to cope with the disturbance to my then dogmatic socialist convictions produced, in 1974, by a reading of Robert Nozick's *Anarchy, State, and Utopia*.

Nozick's political philosophy gains much of its polemical power from the attractive thought that, so it seems to me, constitutes its foundation. That thought is that each person is the morally rightful owner of himself. He possesses over himself, as a matter of moral right, all those rights that a slaveholder has over a complete chattel slave as a matter of legal right, and he is entitled, morally speaking, to dispose over himself in the way such a slaveholder is entitled, legally speaking, to dispose over his slave. Such a slaveholder may not direct his slave to harm other people, but he is not legally obliged to place him at their disposal to the slightest degree: he owes none of his slave's service to anyone else. So, analogously, if I am the moral owner of myself, and therefore of this right arm, then, while others are entitled to prevent it from hitting people, no one is entitled, without my consent, to press it into their own or anybody's else's service, even when my failure to lend it voluntarily to others would be morally wrong.

This last point is important, and it vitiates a certain amount of indignant criticism of Nozick. He does not encourage people not to help one another. Nor does he think that they should not be blamed if they never do so. He merely forbids constrained helping, such as is involved—or so Nozick thinks—in redistributive taxation.[1] He insists that no one enjoys an enforceable noncontractual claim on anyone else's service; or, equivalently, that any enforceable claim on another's service derives from an agreement that binds to the provision of that service. But he does not forbid, or even, Ayn Rand–like, discourage, mutual aid.

1. Robert Nozick, *Anarchy, State, and Utopia* (New York: Basic Books, 1974), p. 169.

Note that the thesis of self-ownership does not say that all that is owned is a self, where "self" is used to denote some particularly intimate, or essential, part of the person. The slaveholder's ownership is not restricted to the self, so construed, of the slave, and the moral self-owner is, similarly, possessed of himself entire, and not of his self alone. The term "self" in the name of the thesis of self-ownership has a purely reflexive significance. It signifies that what owns and what is owned are one and the same, namely, the whole person. There is, consequently, no need to establish that my arm or my power to play basketball well is a proper part of my self, in order for me to claim sovereignty over it under the thesis of self-ownership.

The philosophy I am describing also holds that persons can become, with equally strong moral right, sovereign owners of unequal shares of natural resources, as a result of proper exercises of their own and/ or others' personal powers; and that, when private property in natural resources is rightly generated, its morally privileged origin insulates it against expropriation or limitation. Now a union of self-ownership and unequal distribution of worldly resources readily leads to indefinitely great inequality of private property in external goods of all kinds, and hence to inequality of condition, on any view of what would constitute equality of condition.[2] It follows that inequality of condition is, when properly generated, morally protected, and that the attempt to promote equality of condition at the expense of private property is an unacceptable violation of people's rights. Removing someone's legitimately acquired private property may not be as outrageous as removing his arm, but it is an outrage of the same kind. It is wrong for substantially the same reason.

Now a common left response to Nozick is to recoil from the inequality his view allows, to affirm some sort of equality of condition as a fundamental value, and to reject (at least unqualified) self-ownership

---

2. By "equality of condition" I intend a disjunctive notion, two disjuncts of which are subjected to exceptionally careful study by Ronald Dworkin in "Equality of Welfare" and "Equality of Resources," which appeared in the Summer and Fall issues (respectively) of *Philosophy and Public Affairs*, 1981. As Dworkin notes ("Equality of Welfare," p. 188), other conceptions of equality of condition are possible, but any conception meriting that name is surely incompatible with great inequality of private property in external goods.

because of the inequality of condition it supposedly generates. The conclusion is that people lack the exclusive right to their own powers that goes with self-ownership, and that force may be applied against naturally well-endowed people not only to prevent them from harming others but also to ensure that they help them, so that equality of condition (or not too much inequality of condition) will be secured.

But this line of response to Nozick, in which some sort of equality of condition is affirmed and a denial of self-ownership is derived from it, suffers from two related disadvantages. It has, first, the polemical disadvantage that it is powerless against those who occupy Nozick's position, since they have not failed to notice that their view contradicts (what Nozick would call) the end-state egalitarianism here pressed against it. And the other disadvantage of the stated strategy is that the thesis of self-ownership has, after all, considerable intuitive strength. Its antecedent appeal rivals that of whatever principles of equality it is thought to contradict, even for many committed defenders of such principles: that is why *Anarchy, State, and Utopia* unsettles so many of its liberal and socialist readers.

In my experience, leftists who disparage Nozick's essentially unargued affirmation of each person's rights over himself lose confidence in their unqualified denial of the thesis of self-ownership when they are asked to consider who has the right to decide what should happen to, for example, their own eyes. They do not immediately agree that, were eye transplants easy to achieve, it would then be acceptable for the state to conscribe potential eye donors into a lottery whose losers must yield an eye to beneficiaries who would otherwise be not one-eyed but blind. The fact that they do not deserve their good eyes, that they do not need two good eyes more than blind people need one, and so forth; the fact, in a word, that they are merely lucky to have good eyes does not always convince them that their claim on their own eyes is no stronger than that of some unlucky blind person.[3] But if standard left

3. I am here trying to motivate sympathy for the thesis of self-ownership, not to provide a knock-down argument for it. There are ways of resisting compulsory eye transplanting without affirming (full) self-ownership, but they require more reflection than leftists usually spend on these matters. One way is to hold that noncontractual duties to others begin only once one's own basic needs are satisfied, and that having two eyes is a basic need. Another way is sketched by Ronald Dworkin at pp. 38–39

objections to inequality of resources, private property, and ultimate condition are taken quite literally, then the fact that it is sheer luck that these (relatively) good eyes are mine should deprive me of special privileges in them.

Now one might infer, not that the usual objections to considerable inequality of private property in external things are without force, but that their force is due to the comparative antecedent weakness of the case for exclusive rights in external things. It is an intelligible presumption that I alone am entitled to decide about the use of this arm and to benefit from its dexterity, simply because it is my arm. Nor am I therefore confusing the factual truth that this is my arm with the normative claim that I should have exclusive disposal of it. My contention is that the factual truth is a prima facie plausible basis for, not a logical entailer of, the stated normative claim. But there is no comparable presumptive normative tie between any person and any part or portion of the external world. Hence one may plausibly say of external things, or at any rate of external things in their initial state, of raw land and natural resources (out of which all unraw external things are, of course, made), that no person has a greater prima facie right in them than any other does; whereas the same thought is less compelling when it is applied to human parts and powers. Many have found persuasive the thesis of Rousseau that the original formation of private property was a usurpation of what rightly should be held in common, but few have discerned a comparable injustice in a person's insistence on sovereignty over his own being.

These reflections suggest that those who stand to the left of Nozick might consider a different reaction to him from the one I described earlier. Instead of premising that equality of condition is morally mandatory and rejecting self-ownership on that basis, they might relax their opposition to the idea of self-ownership, but resist its use as the foundation of an argument that proceeds, via a legitimation of inequality in ownership of external resources, to defend the inequality of condition they oppose. They might try to see whether, or to what extent, they can achieve the equality of condition they prize by combining an egal-

---

of his "In Defence of Equality," *Social Philosophy and Policy* (Autumn 1983): 24–40.

itarian approach to worldy resources with an affirmation, or at any rate a nondenial, of the thesis of self-ownership.

I discuss elsewhere economic constitutions that seem to respect both self-ownership and equality of worldly resources.[4] Any such constitution must be opposed both by Nozick and other entitlement theorists on the one hand, and by John Rawls and Ronald Dworkin on the other. For both kinds of theorists are unwilling to distinguish as sharply as might be thought apt between the moral status of ownership of external resources and the moral status of ownership of persons, though they assimilate the two in opposite directions. Nozick endows rightful private ownership of external resources with the moral quality that belongs, more plausibly, to people's ownership of themselves, and Rawls and Dworkin treat people's personal powers as subject, albeit with important qualifications,[5] to the same egalitarian principles of distribution that they apply, less controversially, to external wherewithal. The suggested intermediate position is with Nozick and against Rawls and Dworkin in its affirmation (or at least nondenial) of self-ownership, but with Rawls and Dworkin and against Nozick in regarding the distribution of nonhuman resources as subject to egalitarian appraisal.

Now my present belief is that no such intermediate constitution is capable of ensuring equality of condition, and it follows that the attractive response to Nozick projected two paragraphs back is not, in fact, a viable one. An intermediate constitution preserves self-ownership but equalizes rights in worldly resources. In "Self-Ownership: II" I consider two ways of achieving that latter equalization. One is by placing all external resources under the joint ownership of everyone in society, each having an equal say over what is to be done with them. That provision might, by itself, ensure equality of condition, but it seems to be inconsistent with true self-ownership. For people can do (virtually?) nothing without using parts of the external world. If, then, they require the leave of the community to use it, then, effectively, they do not own themselves, since they can do nothing without com-

---

4. See "Self-Ownership, World-Ownership, and Equality: Part II," forthcoming in *Social Philosophy and Policy*.

5. Rawls and Dworkin assert a certain sovereignty of persons over themselves in their affirmation of political and other liberties, such as choice of career, and granting those liberties has distributive implications.

munal authorization.[6] Hence no truly intermediate constitution will prescribe this first way of equalizing rights in external resources.

Another way of equalizing rights in external resources is by distributing an equal amount of them to each person. Then each, if self-owning, could do with his share as he pleases. This yields a truly intermediate constitution, but one that, I argue, fails to secure the equality of condition socialists prize. I therefore conclude, tentatively, and on the basis of an admittedly incomplete review, that self-ownership and socialist equality are incompatible. Anyone who supports equality of condition must oppose (full) self-ownership, even in a world in which rights over external resources have been equalized.

It follows that Marxists, who surely do support some form of equality of condition, must address the issue of self-ownership more frontally than it is their practice to do. For while Marxists do not, of course, expressly agree with the thesis of self-ownership, they proceed at crucial points as though it were unnecessary for them to disagree with it; unnecessary, that is, to distinguish themselves at a fundamental normative level from left-wing liberals, in a partly natural and partly regimented sense of "left-wing liberals," which I shall now try to define.

Consider three types of entity over which a person might claim sovereignty or (what is here equivalent to it) exclusive private property: the resources of the external world, his own person and powers, and other people. Liberalism, to idealize one of its traditional senses, may be defined as the thesis that each person has full private property in himself (and, consequently, no private property in anyone else). He may do what he likes with himself provided that he does not harm others. Right-wing liberalism, of which Nozick is an exponent, adds, as we have seen, that self-owning persons can acquire equally strong moral rights in external resources. Left-wing liberalism is, by contrast, egalitarian with respect to raw external resources: Henry George, Léon Walras, Herbert Spencer (in his earlier phase), and Hillel Steiner illustrate this position. Rawls and Dworkin are commonly accounted

---

6. The propertyless proletarian who cannot use means of production without a capitalist's leave suffers a similar lack of effective self-ownership. It follows, as I argue in "Self-Ownership: II," that, since Nozick regards proletarianhood as consistent with all the rights he thinks people have, he does not himself, at bottom, defend substantive self-ownership, but something much thinner and far less attractive.

liberals, but here they must be called something else, such as social democrats, for they are not liberals in the traditional sense just defined, since they deny self-ownership in one important way. They say that because it is a matter of brute luck that people have the talents they do, their talents do not, morally speaking, belong to them, but are, properly regarded, resources over which society as a whole may legitimately dispose.

Now Marxists have failed to oppose left-wing liberalism with regard to two large issues, and they have therefore, in respect of those issues, not stood as far left as Rawls and Dworkin do on the spectrum described above, even if one cannot say that they stand to the right of Rawls and Dworkin, since lack of comment by Marxists on the thesis of self-ownership makes it impossible to locate them as definitely as that.

The first issue is the critique of capitalist injustice. In the Marxian version of that critique, the exploitation of workers by capitalists derives entirely from the fact that workers lack access to physical productive resources and must therefore sell their labor power to capitalists, who enjoy a class monopoly in those resources. Hence, for Marxists, the injustice of capitalism is ultimately a matter of unfairness with respect to rights in external things, and its exposure requires no denial of the liberal thesis of self-ownership. Unlike social democrats, who tend to conceive state intervention on behalf of the less well off as securing justified constrained helping, and who must therefore reject the thesis of self-ownership, Marxists regard the badly off as not unlucky but misused, forcibly dispossessed of the means of life, and therefore harmed, and, under that construal of their plight, the demand for its redress needs no foundation stronger than left-wing liberalism.

The second issue is the nature of the ideal society. In the Marxist conception of it external resources are communally owned, as in the leftest of left liberalisms, and the individual is effectively sovereign over himself (even if not as a matter of constitutional right), since the free development of each is, in the famous phrase, the condition of the free development of all. A premise of superfluent abundance makes it unnecessary to press the talent of some into the service of the prosperity of others for the sake of equality of condition.

But Marxist nonopposition to left liberalism on the two issues just described cannot be sustained. Consider, first, the matter of capitalist injustice. What Marxists regard as exploitation will indeed result when people are forcibly denied the external means of producing their existence. One case of that is what Marx called "primitive accumulation," the process whereby, in his account of it, a relatively independent British peasantry was turned into a proletariat by being deprived of its land. But such dispossession, while assuredly a sufficient condition of what Marxists think is exploitation, is not a necessary condition of it. For if all means of production were distributed equally across the population, but people retained self-ownership, then differences in talent and luck and time preference and degrees of willingness to take risk would bring about differential prosperity, which would, in due course, enable some to hire others on Marxian-exploitative terms.[7] Or, to start with a more feasible hypothesis, if all means of production were socially owned and leased to workers' cooperatives for finite periods, then, once again, differences other than ones in initial resource endowments could lead to indefinitely large degrees of inequality of position, and, from there, to Marxian exploitation. So Marxists have exaggerated the extent to which what they consider exploitation depends on an *initial* inequality of rights in worldly assets.

(I digress briefly here to gesture at a problem that I hope to treat more carefully elsewhere. Marxists hold that the value of commodities is constituted entirely by the labor devoted to their production. They deny that worldly resources contribute to the creation of value. The problem is whether that denial is compatible with the extreme importance assigned to worldly resources in the Marxist diagnosis of the root cause of exploitation. Suppose that nature offered up its resources in such a form that there was no reason to alter them by labor. Then, if anything created value, it would have to be nature, or the resources themselves, rather than labor.[8] And only then would an equal distribution of worldly resources virtually ensure the final equality of condition that Marxists favor. To put the point more generally: inequality of condition is the harder to defend precisely to the extent that labor is *not* responsible for the value

7. At least at levels of development of the productive forces below those at which, according to Marxists, capitalism, and therefore capitalist exploitation, will not obtain.

8. I do not myself think that anything, properly speaking, *creates* value, and that is one reason why the point developed in the paragraph above needs more careful statement. Another is that the paragraph pays no attention to the distinction between use value and exchange value, which is relevant here. (For skepticism about the notion of value *creation*, see my "Labour Theory of Value and the Concept of Exploitation," *Philosophy and Public Affairs* 8 [Summer 1979], especially pp. 350, 359).

of commodities. The claim people can make to the fruits of their own labor is the strongest basis for inequality of distribution, and the claim is difficult to reject as long as self-ownership is not denied. There is, then, an apparent discrepancy between the Marxist case for the injustice of capitalism and the Marxist wish to deprecate the significance of nonlabor inputs as a source of value.)

Marxism's nonopposition to left liberalism in the matter of its picture of the good society is also hard to sustain. For confrontation with left liberalism is avoidable only as long as Marxists continue to maintain that abundance will ensure complete compatibility among the interests of differently endowed people, and abundance on the required scale now seems unattainable. A lesser abundance, which enables resolutions of conflicts of interest without coercion, may well be possible.[9] But such resolutions, to secure equality of condition, would lay on the naturally well-endowed obligations to labor for the benefit of those who are not. The former might fulfill their equality-serving obligations without being forced to do so, but they would nevertheless be required to fulfill them as a matter of the constitution of society, and they would, if necessary, be forced to fulfill them, even if (because people would be *sufficiently just and altruistic*)[10] force would never in fact be necessary. And a society that is so constituted violates the principle of self-ownership which is common to all liberalism as liberalism was defined above.

Marxism, then, requires a critique of (left) liberalism. It must develop satisfactory answers to two questions, which it has scarcely raised. The first is, to what extent does a commitment to socialism require rejection of the engaging liberal conception of each person's sovereignty over himself? And the second is, how can rejection of liberalism, to the required extent, be justified?

A provision of answers to those questions would complete my research project, as I currently envisage it. But they will not be dealt

9. Or so I believe, but Marx himself may have been more pessimistic. He seems to have thought that anything short of an abundance that removed all conflicts of interest would guarantee continued social strife, a "struggle for necessities and all the old filthy business" (*The German Ideology* [London, 1965], p. 46). Was it because he was so needlessly pessimistic about anything less than utter abundance that he needed to be so groundlessly optimistic about the possibility of that abundance?

10. They would not have to be *very* just and altruistic because I have premised an abundance that, while smaller than what Marx prophesied, is great enough to ensure that very considerable self-sacrifice for the sake of equality would not be necessary.

with here. My present, more limited task is to argue that whether or not one must, in the end, affirm self-ownership, affirmation of it does not warrant the inegalitarian distribution of worldly resources with which Nozick combines it. This I show by means of a critique of Nozick on appropriation, to which I now turn.

II. Nozick on Appropriation

2. Libertarians, or, to name them more accurately, entitlement theorists,[11] are prone to maintain that the market legitimates the distribution of goods it generates. But every market-generated distribution is only a redistribution of titles that buying and selling are themselves powerless to create, and the upshot of market activity is consequently no more legitimate than the titles with which it operates.[12] But how might the titles that necessarily precede market activity acquire legitimacy in the first place?

The question of what would constitute a rightful original acquisition of private property enjoys a certain priority over the question of what constitutes a rightful subsequent transfer of it, on any definition of private property, since unless private property can be formed, it cannot, a fortiori, be transferred. But, in virtue of the way entitlement theorists define private property, the question of how it may be appropriated should, in their case, have even more priority than it generally does over the question of how it may be transferred. For private property in entitlement discourse is private property in what is sometimes called "the full liberal sense," fitted out with all the rights that could conceivably attach to private property; and once an original acquisition of

11. I argue that they do not deserve the libertarian label at pp. 225–29 of "Illusions about Private Property and Freedom," in John Mepham and David-Hillel Ruben, eds., *Issues in Marxist Philosophy*, vol. 4 (Hassocks, Sussex, 1981). See also pp. 126–27, 134–35 below.

12. As Marx and Spencer noted: " . . . the title itself is simply transferred, and not created by the sale. The title must exist before it can be sold, and a series of sales can no more create this title through continued repetition than a single sale can" (Karl Marx, *Capital* [Moscow, 1962], 3:757). "Does sale or bequest generate a right where it did not previously exist? . . . Certainly not. And if one act of transfer can give no title, can many? No: though *nothing* be multiplied for ever, it will not produce *one*" (Herbert Spencer, *Social Statics* [London, 1851], p. 115).

such robust private property is achieved, then no real problem about its transfer arises, since the full complement of private property rights includes virtually unfettered rights of transfer and bequest. Accordingly, the topic of original appropriation is a most important crux for Nozick's philosophy, and it is therefore startling that he begins his brief discussion of it by remarking that he will now "introduce an additional bit of complexity into the structure of the entitlement theory."[13] That "additional bit" is arguably the most important part of the theory on offer.

Now the problem of initial appropriation would not arise if a certain false thing that Nozick says earlier were true, namely, that "things come into the world already attached to people having entitlements over them."[14] That is relevantly false, since people create nothing ex nihilo, and all external private property either is or was made of something that was once no one's private property, either in fact or morally (or was made of something that was made of something that was once not private property, or was made of something that was made of something that was made of something that was once not private property, and so on).[15] In the prehistory of any existing piece of private property there was at least one moment at which something privately unowned was taken into private ownership. If, then, someone claims a Nozick-like right to something he legally owns, we may ask, apart from how he in particular came to own it, with what right it came to be *anyone's* private property in the first place.

Now it is easy to doubt that much actually existing private property was formed in what entitlement theorists could plausibly claim was a legitimating way. But let us here set aside questions about actual history. Let us ask, instead, by what means, if any, full liberal private property *could* legitimately be formed.

13. Nozick, *Anarchy, State, and Utopia*, p. 174.
14. Ibid., p. 160.
15. Hillel Steiner formulates the essential point as follows: "It is a necessary truth that no object can be made from nothing, and hence that all titles to manufactured or freely transferred objects must derive from titles to natural and previously unowned objects" ("Justice and Entitlement," in Jeffrey Paul, ed., *Reading Nozick* [Totowa, N.J.: Rowman & Littlefield, 1981], p. 381). See, too, his "Natural Right to the Means of Production," *Philosophical Quarterly* 27 (1977): 44. Nozick himself recognizes the relevant truth elsewhere: "Since as far back as we know, everything comes from something else, to find an origin is to find a relative beginning, the beginning of an entity as being of a certain kind *K*" (*Philosophical Explanations* [Oxford, 1981], p. 660 [11]).

Nozick's answer to that question is part of his total theory of justice in holdings. According to that theory, a distribution of property is to be defended or criticized not in the light of considerations of need or reward for effort or the like, but by reference to information about the whole past history of the objects in the distribution.[16] With respect to a given item of private property, we obtain the required information when we learn whether or not its owner acquired it justly, either from nature (call such acquisition *appropriation*) or from another who held it justly, because he in turn similarly acquired it justly from nature or from another who held it justly, because he in turn . . . (and so on, as before). Just holding depends on originally just appropriation and subsequently just transfer, except where the holding is a result of redistribution justified by injustice in past acts of appropriation and/or transfer.

Nozick devotes nine densely packed pages to the topic of just appropriation. Considering how important appropriation is for his theory, and bearing in mind Nozick's powers of exposition and advocacy, the pages are remarkably unsatisfactory. I do not mean merely that it is possible to criticize Nozick's argument, though that is certainly true. I mean that the pages are wanting in two more purely expository respects. First, Nozick distinguishes awkwardly between various provisos on acquisition without noting other noteworthy provisos that belong to the same conceptual area, and, as a result, without producing agreeably exclusive and exhaustive distinctions.[17] And, second, it is not always

16. Information of the required kind is, of course, to a large extent inaccessible, and this makes it hard to derive policy implications from Nozick's theory, but it is not obvious that it weakens the theory itself, since it might belong to the nature of justice that it is typically very hard to tell whether or not an existing distribution of property is just. (Compare the argument sometimes wrongly thought to be decisive against utilitarianism, that it is impossible in practice to determine in advance—or even in arrears—the comparative consequences of available courses of action.)

17. Here is a partial justification of that charge. (Nonaficionados of Nozick exegesis may profitably ignore this footnote, for which his p. 176 is required reading.) At p. 176 of *Anarchy, State, and Utopia*, Nozick contrasts two ways in which "someone may be made worse off by another's appropriation": "first, by losing the opportunity to improve his situation by a particular appropriation or any one; and second, by no longer being able to use freely (without appropriation) what he previously could." He then proceeds to distinguish between a "stringent" (here called S) and a "weaker" (W) proviso on acquisition. Call the appropriator A and any person whose position might

clear when he is supposed to be expounding Locke and when developing his own position. He is not utterly forthright about how satisfactory he thinks various provisos on acquisition are. It is consequently hard to know how much he thinks he achieves in these critically important

---

be worsened by *A*'s appropriation *B*. Then *W* and *S* may be formulated as follows:

    W: *A* must not cause *B* to lose the opportunity to use freely what he previously could.

    S: *W*, and *A* must not cause *B* to lose the opportunity to improve his situation by appropriating something, unless *B* is adequately compensated for any such loss of opportunity.

Now *S* is a conjunction, one conjunct of which is *W*, and the rest of which I shall call *S'*. Then note that *S'* differs from *W* in three independent ways. First, *S'* focuses on *B*'s opportunities to appropriate things, whereas *W* focuses on his opportunities to use them. Second, *S'* requires that *B* not lose opportunities to *improve* his situation, whereas *W* does not mention possible improvements and therefore presumably forbids only making *B* worse off than he was, and not (also) making him worse off than he would or might have become. And, finally, *S'* contains a compensation clause ("unless . . . "), whereas *W* does not. (Nozick may wrongly have thought that *B* could improve his condition only by appropriating something, and, also wrongly, that no compensation could be added to *W*; in which case the three differences between *S'* and *W* would not be independent.)

Both the second and third differences have consequences unnoticed by Nozick, but I shall here fix on the third difference only, that *S'* has and *W* lacks a compensation clause. It has the effect that *W* is weaker than *S* only because *W* is a conjunct of *S*, and not also because, as Nozick surely thought, *W* is weaker than *S'*. *W* is not weaker than *S'*, since the compensation clause in *S'* generates a way of satisfying *S'* without satisfying *W*.

I think Nozick has confused the difference between *W* and *S'* with the difference between *S'* and *S''*, *S''* being *S* shorn of both *W* and the compensation clause:

    S'':   *A* must not cause *B* to lose the opportunity to improve his situation by appropriating something.

Here are three reasons for thinking that Nozick has confused the *W*/*S'* and *S'*/*S''* differences:

(a) Nozick distinguishes between *S* and *W* in order to meet a regress argument he presents at p. 176 and to which the reader is referred. He says that *S* generates the regress and *W* does not. But it is not true that *S* generates the regress: its compensation clause offers appropriators the possibility of compensating those who can no longer appropriate, and therefore permits the final appropriation prohibition of which is necessary to get the regress going. It is *S''*, not *S'* (or, hence, *S*), that makes the regress inescapable.

(b) On p. 178 Nozick states a proviso which I quote below and which, he says, is "similar to the weaker of the ones we have attributed to Locke." But the p. 178 proviso resembles not *W* but *S'*, its relative weakness being due solely to its compensation clause.

pages. But what matters most, of course, is how much he in fact achieves, whatever he may think.

Nozick interprets Locke conventionally, as holding that an agent may appropriate what he mixes his labor with, provided that he leaves enough and as good for others and does not waste what he takes. He comments skeptically on the labor mixture notion, expresses puzzlement at Locke's insistence that appropriators must avoid waste, and spends most of his time discussing and refining the provision that they must leave enough and as good for others.

I think Nozick is right to concentrate his attention on the "enough and as good" provision. For objection to an appropriation is more likely to fix on its impact on others than on the means whereby it was brought about. And if, in particular, its impact on others is harmless, as satisfaction of Locke's provision would seem to ensure, then it will be difficult to criticize it, regardless of how it was effected, and even, therefore, if no labor was expended in the course of it. It is, moreover, worth remarking that some of Locke's most plausible examples of legitimate appropriation cannot reasonably be said to result from labor, unless all acting on the world is regarded as laboring. For even on a reasonably broad view of what labor is, picking up a few fallen acorns and immersing one's head in a stream and swallowing some of its water are not good examples of it.[18] Or, if they are indeed labor, then they are not labor that it would be plausible to cite in defense of the relevant appropriations. If you were asked what justified your appropriation of the water from the stream, you could not credibly reply: "Well, to begin with, the labor of dunking my head and opening my mouth." Your powerful reply is to say that no one has good reason to complain about your appropriation of the water, since no one is negatively affected by it.

(c) Whereas W indeed invalidates the regress argument, it does forbid transformation of all common land into private property, at least if some end up with no private property. But in the kind of capitalist society that Nozick thinks defensible just such privatization of all common land has occurred, and there exist propertyless people without access to anything still held in common. Therefore W cannot serve Nozick's polemical purposes, whereas S', because of its compensation clause, can.

18. See pars. 28, 29, and 33 of the *Second Treatise of Government*. (Par. 33 is given in full below.)

So I agree with Nozick that "the crucial point is whether an appropriation of an unowned object worsens the situation of others."[19] Disagreement will come on the question of what should here count as worsening another's situation.

Nozick refines the crucial condition as follows: "A process normally giving rise to a permanent bequeathable property right in a previously unowned thing will not do so if the position of others no longer at liberty to use the thing is thereby worsened."[20] He makes no attempt to specify the nature of the "normal" acquisition process, but, as I just suggested, that is not very important, since, whatever process is required, controversy is likely to settle on the provision just quoted. Hence, although it is not so billed,[21] with the quoted statement, with Nozick's elaboration of it, *is* Nozick's doctrine of appropriation; or, more cautiously, if Nozick presents any doctrine of appropriation, then the quoted statement is the element in his doctrine which needs special scrutiny.

Nozick's further discussion justifies the following comments on his proviso. It requires of an appropriation of an object O, which was unowned and available to all, that its withdrawal from general use does not make anyone's prospects worse than they would have been *had O remained in general use*. If no one's position is in any way made worse than it would have been had O remained unowned, then, of course, the proviso is satisfied. But it is also satisfied when someone's position is in some relevant way worsened, as long as his position is in other ways sufficiently improved to counterbalance that worsening. Hence I appropriate something legitimately if and only if no one has any reason to prefer its remaining in general use, or whoever does have some reason to prefer that gets something in the new situation which he did not have before and which is worth at least as much to him as what I have caused him to lose. To illustrate: I enclose the beach, which has

19. Nozick, *Anarchy, State, and Utopia*, p. 175.
20. Ibid., p. 178.
21. Or perhaps it is so billed. For Nozick's pages on appropriation begin, as I reported earlier, with the announcement that "an additional bit of complexity" must now be introduced "into the structure of the entitlement theory" and end with an announcement that "this completes our indication of the complication in the entitlement theory introduced by the Lockean proviso" (ibid., pp. 174, 182). If the "complexity" of p. 174 is the "complication" of p. 182, then the condition on appropriation stated on p. 178 *is* Nozick's theory of appropriation, at least insofar as he has one.

been common land, declare it my own, and announce a price of one dollar per person per day for the use of it (or, if you think there could not be dollars in what sounds like a state of nature situation, then imagine that my price is a certain amount of massage of my bad back). But I so enhance the recreational value of the beach (perhaps by dyeing the sand different attractive colours, or just by picking up the litter every night) that all would-be users of it regard a dollar (or a massage) for a day's use of it as a dollar well spent: they prefer a day at the beach as it now is in exchange for a dollar to a free day at the beach as it was and as it would have remained had no one appropriated it. Hence my appropriation of the beach satisfies Nozick's proviso.

Now it might seem that appropriations satisfying Nozick's condition could not conceivably generate a grievance. But that is an illusion. For Nozick's proviso on acquisition is not as demanding as Locke's. To see how Locke intended his proviso, and how solicitous it is toward nonappropriators, consider paragraph 33 of the *Second Treatise*:

> Nor was this appropriation of any parcel of land, by improving it, any prejudice to any other man, since there was still enough and as good left; and more than the yet unprovided could use. So that in effect there was never the less left for others because of his enclosure for himself. For he that leaves as much as another can make use of, does as good as take nothing at all. Nobody could think himself injured by the drinking of another man, though he took a good draught, who had a whole river of the same water left to quench his thirst; and the case of land and water, where there is enough of both, is perfectly the same.[22]

22. Locke's proviso does not mean what Steiner says it means when he writes that "it imposes an egalitarian structure on individuals' appropriative entitlements, prescribing to each a quantitatively and qualitatively similar bundle of natural objects" ("Natural Right," p. 45). One must leave for others enough and as good to use and/or appropriate *as they had before one appropriated*, not enough and as good to appropriate, *per capita, as one appropriates oneself*. Satisfaction of Locke's provision entails satisfaction of the provision Steiner misattributes to him, but the converse entailment fails, and Locke's provision is therefore more stringent than the one Steiner states. (I grant that Locke notes, at paragraph 34, that legitimate appropriators satisfy what Steiner thinks is Locke's proviso, since Locke says that, in the wake of a legitimate appropriation, nonappropriators have "as good left for [their] improvement as was already taken up." But it does not follow that this entailment of what I say is Locke's proviso *is* his proviso, and I think it textually demonstrable that it is not.)

If people must leave for others resources as good as they had available to them before, then what is added by the apparently further stipulation that they leave them enough?

Note that there is no way at all in which anyone might have been or become better off had the man not drunk that water: as far as others are concerned, his drinking it leaves things exactly as they were. They would not have been better off even if he had given them the water he took, since the stream, we are to imagine, flowed so abundantly that, even if they wanted water, they did not need his.[23]

But whereas people cannot be made worse off than they might have been by an appropriation that satisfies Locke's proviso, the same is not true of Nozick's. People can be made seriously worse off than they might have been, even when it is fulfilled. That is because of the phrase I had occasion to italicize earlier: *"had O remained in general use."* It has the upshot that, as Nozick intends his proviso, *the only counterfactual situation relevant to assessing the justice of an appropriation is one in which O would have continued to be accessible to all.*[24] I shall argue that there are other intuitively relevant counterfactuals, and that they show that Nozick's condition is too lax. The possibilities I shall review compose a decisive case against Nozick's theory of private

---

"Enough" presumably means "enough to survive by the use of," but if resources as good as were previously available are left, then the "enough" stipulation is unsatisfied only if others already lacked enough to live on. It is therefore difficult to see what the force of the "enough" stipulation is.

23. Locke's drinker satisfies a proviso even stronger than Locke's, and one that Nozick's medical researcher (*Anarchy, State, and Utopia*, p. 181), who satisfies Locke's proviso, does not satisfy. That researcher makes a much-needed drug, which no one else knows how to make out, of resources in superfluent supply, and therefore makes no one worse off than he was before by so doing. But, unlike Locke's water taker, he could benefit others, namely, those who need the drug, by giving it to them or selling it to them cheaply. Locke's proviso allows one to take and transform and keep what others had no need of in its untransformed state, even if they need it once it has been transformed. A stronger proviso, satisfied by the water taker but not by the researcher, would allow one to take and transform and keep only what no one had reason to want even after it had been transformed. (Nozick's researcher, in satisfying Locke's proviso, thereby satisfies a proviso much stronger than Nozick's. It is important to notice that, for otherwise Nozick's proviso might look more innocent than it is.)

24. At p. 181 of *Anarchy, State, and Utopia* Nozick in effect acknowledges that to consider only that counterfactual situation makes the "baseline" above which people must be for private property to be justified very low. (How, by the way, does his confident remark about the baseline on p. 181 square with his expression of agnosticism about its proper height at p. 177? Is he speaking about different baselines, or is one of those two remarks a slip? If different baselines are in issue, I do not understand what the difference between them is.)

property formation, and a case, be it noted, which raises no challenge to the thesis of self-ownership.

3.   To see how Nozick's condition operates, and to test it, imagine a two-person world in which there is, initially, Lockean common ownership of its finite quantity of land. Each of the self-owning persons, who are A and B, draws sustenance from the land without obstructing the sustenance-drawing activity of the other. A is able to get m from the land, and B is able to get n, where m and n are, let us say, numbers of bushels of wheat (or, if you think individual wheat production hard to achieve on common land, think of m and n as numbers of gallons of cows' milk, or, better, of moose milk, taken from moose that neither A nor B owns). One might say that m and n represent what A and B are able to obtain through exercise of the personal powers each separately owns under common ownership of the land. Note that the relative sizes of m and n, which reflect the relative personal powers of A and B, will play no role in the reasoning to follow.

Now suppose that A appropriates all the land, or—this being the theoretically crucial amount—an amount that leaves B less than enough to live off. He then offers B a salary of $n + p$ $(p \geq 0)$ bushels to work the land, which B perforce accepts. A himself gets $m + q$ under the new arrangement, and q is greater than p, so that A gains more extra bushels from the change than B does. In other words, B loses no wheat and maybe gains some, but in any case A gains more than B does. The rise in output, from $n + m$ to $n + m + p + q$, is due to the productivity of a division of labor designed by A, who is a good organizer. Let us call the situation following A's appropriation the *actual situation*. It is the situation with which we shall compare various counterfactual ones. (The relevant features of the situations to be discussed will be found in Table 1.)

Now does A's appropriation satisfy Nozick's proviso? To see whether it does, we must compare B's condition after A's appropriation with how B would have fared had common ownership persisted, and, for simplicity's sake, let us suppose that B would have fared exactly as he was already faring: he would have continued to draw just n bushels of wheat. Then A's appropriation clearly satisfies Nozick's condition, *if* the way to reckon the change in B's prospects is by comparing numbers of bushels of wheat. If, however, being subject to the directives of another person is regarded as a relevant effect on B of A's appropriation,

Table 1

	Actual situation (A's appropriation)	I. Persistence of common ownership	II. B's appropriation		
			(*a*) B's talent $=$ A's talent	(*b*) B's talent $>$ A's talent	(*c*) B's talent $<$ A's talent
A gets	$m + q$	m	$m + p$	$m + q + r$	m
B gets	$n + p$	n	$n + q$	$n + p + s$	n
	$(q > p \geq 0)$			$(r > 0; s > 0)$	

then we cannot say whether or not the latter violates Nozick's proviso, since we have not put a value on the disbenefit to B of being under A's command. In assessing the gains and losses people sustain following transformations such as the one we are examining, entitlement theorists tend to neglect the value people may place on the kind of power relations in which they stand to others,[25] a neglect that is extraordinary in supposed libertarians professedly committed to human autonomy and the overriding importance of being in charge of one's own life. I shall, however, make no further use of this point in my demonstration of the inadequacy of Nozick's theory of private property formation.[26] I shall henceforth assess benefit and disbenefit in terms of nothing but numbers of bushels of wheat.

To see that Nozick's condition on appropriation is too weak, consider now a different counterfactual situation, not that in which common use persists but one in which B, perhaps concerned lest A do so, appropriates what A appropriates in the actual situation. Suppose that B is also a good organizer, and that had he appropriated *he* could have got an additional q and paid A only an additional p (see IIa in Table 1). Then although A's appropriation in the actual situation satisfies Nozick's proviso,[27] it does not seem that A has what he does have on Nozick's

25. See my "Robert Nozick and Wilt Chamberlain: How Patterns Preserve Liberty," in John Arthur and William Shaw, eds., *Justice and Economic Distribution* (Englewood Cliffs, N.J.: Prentice-Hall, 1978), pp. 251–53, 258–60; and Michael Walzer, *Spheres of Justice* (New York: Basic Books, 1983), pp. 291–303.

26. The point is central to the further criticism of Nozick mounted in "Self-Ownership: II" and briefly indicated in n. 6 above.

27. If, that is, B's loss of liberty is ignored: see the previous paragraph in the text.

view, the right to force B to accept it. For why should B be required to accept what amounts to a doctrine of "first come, first served"? Perhaps B abstained from appropriating out of regard for A. Ought A to profit only because he is more ruthless than B? It should now be clear that Nozick's proviso is too weak.

Other possibilities[28] make this clearer still. To take one of them, suppose that B is a much better organizer than A so that, had B appropriated, then each of A and B would have had more wheat than he does in the actual situation (see IIb in Table I). Nozick's proviso is, nevertheless, satisfied, since whether or not it is satisfied is unaffected by anything that might have happened had B appropriated. And this means that Nozick's condition licenses and protects appropriations whose upshots make each person worse off than he need be, upshots that are, therefore, in one good sense, Pareto-inferior.[29] A, if sufficiently ignorant or irrational to do so, would be entitled to prevent B from taking what A had appropriated, even if both would become better off if B took it.

In constructing the "actual situation" I supposed that the productivity increase it displayed was due to A's organizational talent. But that supposition was unnecessary, and, if we suppose otherwise, then the case against Nozick is seen to be even stronger. Suppose, then, that B alone is a good organizer, and that, when A has appropriated, he proposes to B that B design an optimal division of labor and then play his role in it, for the same $n + p$ wage, and that B, preferring exploitation to starvation, accepts. Then A's appropriation is still justified under Nozick's proviso, even though here it is the case not merely that B could also have engineered a productivity gain but that he actually

28. Not, that is, different counterfactual situations, but different possible upshots of the same counterfactual situation.

29. Pareto-inferiority is an ambiguous notion among economists, who tend not to distinguish between the idea that everyone would *favor* a different situation and the idea that everyone would *benefit from* a different situation (whatever they may themselves think and hence favor whatever they are inclined to favor). I am using the Pareto notion in the second of these two ways, and what I say is false when it is taken in the first way.

Nozick himself sometimes allows (what would otherwise be?) violations of rights to secure a Pareto-improvement in the present sense, but only when communication with unconsenting but benefiting persons is impossible. See the last full sentence on p. 72 of *Anarchy, State, and Utopia*. But see, too, Eric Mack, "Nozick on Unproductivity," in Paul, ed., *Reading Nozick*, for an argument that Nozick's selective permission of "boundary crossings" with compensation threatens to unfound his defense of the sanctity of private property.

is the one who brings it about. The example shows that, even when privatization generates additional value, the privatizer need not be the real value adder, and, if one thinks that value adders merit reward,[30] then one should note that Nozick's condition does not ensure that they get any. To reap all the benefit from any enhancement of production that results from privatization, his just appropriators need not do anything to resources beyond making them their own.

I also supposed that the productive division of labor in force in the actual situation and in II*a* and II*b*, could not have been implemented under Lockean common ownership. That seems to me true by definition. To be sure, *A* and *B* might have agreed to a division of labor without either of them privately appropriating the land. But then, so I would argue, they would, in effect, have appropriated it collectively. They would have instituted a form of socialism, which is another possibility unjustifiably neglected by Nozick, and about which I shall say more in section 4.

But now suppose that *B* lacks *A*'s organizational powers, and that, if he had appropriated the land, he could not have so directed *A* as to generate any increase over what gets produced under common ownership (see II*c* of Table 1). Under that assumption, is *A*'s appropriation justified?

It is justified only if ($\neq$if and only if) we should not regard the land as *jointly owned* at the outset. When land is owned in common, each can use it on his own initiative, provided that he does not interfere with similar use by others: under common ownership of the land no one owns any of it. Under joint ownership, by contrast, the land *is* owned, by all together, and what each may do with it is subject to collective decision. The appropriate procedure for reaching that decision may be hard to define, but it will certainly not be open to any one of the joint owners to privatize all or part of the asset unilaterally, no matter what compensation he offers to the rest. If you and I jointly own a house, I cannot, against your will, section off a third of it and leave you the rest, even if what I leave is worth more than your share in the whole was. So if joint ownership rather than no ownership is, morally speak-

30. I am not myself here affirming that they do: one need not suppose that value adders should get (some of) the value of what they produce in order to regard them as exploited by those who get it just because they have power over them. See my "Labor Theory of Value," p. 357, n. 21, par. 2.

ing, the original position,[31] then B has the right to forbid A to appropriate, even if B would benefit by what he thereby forbids. And B might have good reasons to exercise his right to forbid an appropriation by A from which B himself would benefit. For, if he forbids A to appropriate, he can then bargain with A about the share of output he will get if he relents and allows A to appropriate. B is then likely to improve his take by an amount greater than what A would otherwise have offered him.

So Nozick must suppose that the world's resources are, morally speaking, nothing like jointly owned, but very much up for grabs, yet, far from establishing that premise, he does not even bother to state it, or show any awareness that he needs it.

4.   In the section of *Anarchy, State, and Utopia* which precedes the one in which he states the proviso criticized above, Nozick asks and answers a question that is germane to that proviso, although it is obscure whether or not he has that very proviso in mind when he puts the question. The question is whether "the situation of persons [like our B] who are unable to appropriate (there being no more accessible and useful unowned objects) [is] worsened by a system allowing appropriation and permanent property."[32] Nozick intends thereby to ask whether such people are worse off than they would have been had such a system never developed. His question is roughly equivalent to the question whether the existence of capitalism makes noncapitalists better off than they otherwise would have been.

Nozick replies by marshaling some familiar empirical theses about the utility of private property, the usual claims about risks, incentives, and so forth which represent capitalism as a productive form of economic organization. But, as he points out, he does not invoke these considerations to provide a utilitarian justification of private property, for here they

31. For a partial explication of the idea of joint ownership of the world by all of its inhabitants, and a defense of it against what seem at first to be fatal objections, see John Exdell, "Distributive Justice: Nozick and Property Rights," *Ethics* 87 (January 1977), especially pp. 147–49. The idea is more or less explicit in various articles by Hillel Steiner; see, for example, his "Liberty and Equality," *Political Studies* 34 (1980): 555–69, and "The Rights of Future Generations," in Douglas MacLean and Peter G. Brown, eds., *Energy and the Future* (Totowa, N.J.: Rowman & Littlefield, 1983), pp. 225–41.

32. Nozick, *Anarchy, State, and Utopia*, p. 177.

"enter a Lockean theory to support the claim that appropriation of private property satisfies the intent behind the 'enough and as good left over' proviso."[33] When there is nothing left to appropriate, the situation of those who have appropriated nothing is to that extent worse than it would have been, but the mechanisms of production and distribution under capitalism ensure that they are more than adequately compensated for their loss of freedom of access to resources that are not privately owned.

As explained, the empirical claims about the utility of private property figure here in an argument whose major premise is not utilitarianism. The argument is not: whatever makes people better off is a good thing, and private property makes people better off; but: anyone has the right to appropriate private property when that makes nobody worse off, and appropriation of private property in general makes everyone better off (and therefore not worse off). And Nozick's conclusion, unlike the utilitarian one, is not that a private property system, being best, should be brought into being or, if it exists, kept. It is that if a private property system exists, then the fact that some people own no or little private property in it is not a reason for removing it. (He would say, of those propertyless persons who are forced to sell their labor power, that they will get more in exchange for it from their employers than they could have hoped to get by applying it in a rude state of nature; and, of those propertyless persons whose labor power is not worth buying, that, though they may therefore die, they would have died in the state of nature anyway.)

Even so, because he depends on an empirical minor premise, Nozick's defense of private property turns out to be, like the utilitarian defense of it, potentially vulnerable to empirical counterargument. His major premise is not empirical, but neither is the major premise of the utilitarian defense, which is that whatever makes people better off is a good thing. I point this out because it is often thought to be an attraction of Nozick's political philosophy that, through its emphasis on rights, it finesses empirical questions about consequences which are hard to answer and in which utilitarianism becomes enmired. That is an illusion, since, as we now see, theses about consequences are foundational to Nozick's defense of private property rights, and the rights he asserts consequently lack the clarity and authority he would like us to suppose they have.

33. Ibid.

G. A. Cohen

Nozick's empirical claims are addressed and rebutted, one by one, by Hal Varian, who argues that "market socialist" or "people's capitalistic" property arrangements are more productive still than the pure capitalism Nozick favors, at any rate under certain conditions.[34]

But it is not clear that Varian's empirical counterclaims touch the case for capitalism which Nozick builds at page 177, as Nozick intends that case. For Varian compares the regime of capitalist private property not to unstructured common ownership but to an organized non- or merely semicapitalist property system. And if institutionally undeveloped common ownership is the only thing to which we are supposed to compare capitalism when we seek an answer to the question quoted in the first paragraph of this section, as it is indeed the only thing we are allowed to consider when testing Nozick's proviso, then Varian's remarks are, in an immediate sense, beside the point. But only in an immediate sense. For if Varian's counterclaims are irrelevant in the way suggested, then that is only because Nozick is, once again, unreasonably restricting the range of permissible comparison. For why should institutionally primitive common ownership be the only alternative to capitalism which is allowed to count, and not also more structured noncapitalist arrangements? Yet, if the latter are indeed allowed to count, then Nozick's confidence in his case for capitalism, and his blithe certainty that capitalism satisfies his proviso,[35] may be judged to be unfounded. When assessing A's appropriation we should consider not only what would have happened had B appropriated, but also what would have happened had A and B cooperated under a socialist economic constitution.[36]

Now once we broaden, in these and other ways, our range of comparison, then, so it seems, a defensibly strong Lockean proviso will

34. See Hal Varian, "Distributive Justice, Welfare Economics, and the Theory of Fairness," *Philosophy and Public Affairs* 4 (Spring 1975): 235, 237–38. Another theorist of appropriation who emphasizes the advantages of capitalism over the Lockean state of nature without noting that a noncapitalist system might be more advantageous still is Baruch Brody. See his "Redistribution without Egalitarianism," *Social Philosophy and Policy* (Autumn 1983), especially p. 82.

35. Expressed at p. 181 (see n. 24 above): that certainty depends on regarding Lockean common ownership as the only alternative with which capitalism need be compared.

36. And, too, what would have happened had there been an equal division of the land rather than Nozickian appropriation.

forbid the formation of full liberal private property. For there will always be some who would have been better off under an alternative dispensation that it would be arbitrary to exclude from consideration. (An example of an alternative dispensation that it would *not* be arbitrary to exclude is that in which everyone is the slave of the tallest person in the society.) And since, moreover, a defensibly strong Lockean proviso on the formation and retention of economic systems will rule that no one should be worse off in the given economic system than he would have been under some unignorable alternative, it almost certainly follows that not only capitalism but every economic system will fail to satisfy a defensibly strong Lockean proviso, and that one must therefore abandon the Lockean way of testing the legitimacy of economic systems.

One alternative is to settle for utilitarianism. Because of its aggregative character, utilitarianism is insensitive to the fate of the individual, and it therefore has no use for Lockean provisos. But if, like Nozick and myself, one regards utilitarianisms as consistent with monstrous violation of individual rights, then a different alternative is necessary.

One different alternative is John Rawls's difference principle, in its strict meaning, which contrasts with the way many, including, I think, Rawls, often misinterpret it. In its strict meaning the difference principle is satisfied by a given economic system only if those who are worst off under it are not more badly off than the worst off would be under any alternative to it. But since those who are actually worst off need not be those who would be worst off in an alternative system, the difference principle may be satisfied even if those actually worst off would be better off in that alternative. The difference principle is therefore not, as it may falsely appear to be, a Lockean proviso whose range is restricted to the worst off, and it can be satisfied even when such a proviso is not satisfied. But the difference principle has an intuitive power comparable to that of a Lockean proviso. For when it is satisfied one may respond to the complaint of the worst-off group by pointing out that others would suffer at least as much as they do in any dispensation in which they were better off than they actually are.

Now Rawls seems sometimes to interpret the difference principle as though the worst off in an economy that satisfies it would *themselves* be no better off under any alternative.[37] He seems so to interpret it

37. This misconstrual is manifest at p. 103 and fairly evident at p. 536 of *A Theory*

when he urges the immunity of a society that satisfies it to instability through unrest from below, for in an economy that satisfies the difference principle in its incorrect form the worst off would indeed have no reason for unrest. But this involves a misinterpretation of the difference principle, since the latter is chosen in the original position, whose occupants must treat ''worst-off group'' as a nonrigid designator.

The misinterpreted difference principle *is* a strong Lockean proviso, with its range restricted to those who are worst off. So misinterpreted, the principle is, like unrestricted Lockean provisos, almost certainly unsatisfiable. The difference principle proper can, however, be satisfied, and it is to that extent superior to a Lockean test of economic systems, once the whole feasible set of them is brought into view.

5. I have argued elsewhere that the familiar idea that private property and freedom are conceptually connected is an ideological illusion.[38] In the light of Nozick's doctrine of appropriation, I am able to provide further support for that claim.

Call an action *paternalist* if it is performed for the sake of another's benefit but against his will, and if it actually does benefit him as intended. A state that imposes a health insurance scheme on people all of whom benefit from it but some of whom are, on whatever basis, opposed to it acts paternalistically in the defined sense (if, as I am supposing, the state applies the scheme to those who do not want it

---

of Justice (Cambridge: Belknap Press of Harvard University Press, 1971). Why does Rawls commit it? An unkind speculation would be that he tacitly supposes that the worse off in any given economic system are by nature so constituted that they would be the worst off in every one. Or perhaps he conflates the truth that the worst off in a system that satisfies the difference principle would, necessarily, be even worse off under flat equality with the falsehood that they would, necessarily, be the worst off under any other system.

To see the distinction between the difference principle proper and its misconstrual, suppose that a society is in state *A* and that *B* is the only feasible alternative to it:

	A	B
Jack	10	10
Jill	8	5
Mary	6	9

(The numbers represent amounts of primary goods.) The difference principle mandates retention of *A*, its misconstrual a change to *B*.

38. In the article referred to in n. 11 above.

for their own good, and not, for example, because the scheme is a public good and the state is against free riding). Nozick would say that the scheme is unjust, because the taxation it levies, like all taxation whose purpose is not to protect property rights, violates property rights. He would, a fortiori, regard as unjust a policy that taxes someone against his will and that in fact benefits him, even though it is not intended to benefit him: we can call that an *objectively paternalist* policy. Note that the Nozickian objection we are here considering is not that there is a constrained transfer from one person to another, that, for example, nobody should be forced to pay for anyone else's health care. Nozick would object even if the amount of tax a person paid were strictly related to his own health prospects.

Nozick disallows objectively paternalist use of people's private property.[39] But he permits objectively paternalist treatment of people in other ways. For since he permits appropriations that satisfy nothing but his proviso, he allows A to appropriate against B's will when B benefits as a result, or rather as long as B does not lose.[40]

Are Nozick's positions consistent? He would say that they are, since B's rights are not violated when A appropriates, and rights are violated when the state funds a medical plan through taxation. And that is so, *if* Nozick's theory of appropriation and property rights is correct, but it would seem question-begging to allow that theory to establish the mooted consistency here, where we are examining Nozick's attempt to ground property rights in the first place. And whether or not the move would be question-begging, it is clear beyond doubt that an appropriation of private property can contradict an individual's will just as much as levying a tax on him can.[41] Therefore Nozick cannot claim to be inspired throughout by a desire to protect freedom, unless he means by ''freedom'' what he really does mean by it: the freedom of private property owners to do as they wish with their property.

39. The special case mentioned in n. 29 above is not a counterexample to that statement, since what Nozick there allows is benefiting someone not against his known will but merely without his known compliance.

40. Actually, he permits still more, since he allows B to be made worse off than he would have been, as long as he is not made worse off than he would have become under persistence of common ownership. But that point was made in sec. 3, and I am here setting it aside in order to focus on the present different one.

41. The point that formation of private property can contradict a person's (such as B's) will should not be confused with the point I made earlier, that it can turn one person into another's subordinate.

[6]

Justice Here and Now

Michael Walzer

For most intellectual purposes, we draw a line between philosophical speculation about politics and actual political debate. It is conceivably a useful line, but it is also an artificial and sometimes a misleading line. For philosophy reflects and articulates the political culture of its time, and politics presents and enacts the arguments of philosophy. Of course, one-eyed philosophers distort what they reflect, and simple-minded and partisan politicians mutilate what they enact, but there can be no doubt about the two-way movement. Philosophy is politics reflected upon in tranquillity, and politics is philosophy acted out in confusion. The link between the two, the connection of theory to practice, was once thought to be a special concern of the left: it was the goal of the left to overcome the division of labor between philosophers and politicians, to impose upon philosophers something of the immediacy of political struggle so as to give them a chance at something like the pleasure of political victory. Leftist writers were prepared to intensify present confusions for the sake of future tranquillities. But the clearest contemporary example of the connection between philosophy and politics comes from the right: market ideology and its immediate companion, the new politics of laissez-faire.

This same example also provides wonderful material for the study of one-eyed philosophers and simple-minded and partisan politicians. For market ideology is a highly distorted reflection of our political culture, ignoring or repressing examples of communal cooperation and state action and denying the significance of political struggles for public health, industrial democracy, workplace safety, environmental control, and so on. And laissez-faire politics has taken the form of a crude attack on the welfare state, leaving the large-scale public subsidy of capitalist enterprise untouched. But I don't want to elaborate these commonplace criticisms except incidentally in the course of a rather different and more positive project. I shall try to address some of the issues that figure in current political debates and to describe what I take to be the necessary features of distributive justice in the United States today. It is important to stress that last prepositional phrase: in the United States today, that is, among ourselves, given our lives, values, and common practices. It is my purpose here not to make universal pronouncements but to reflect upon the real and particular pluralism of American culture and to suggest the pattern of social policy that follows from that pluralism. How must we live together if we are not to oppress and injure one another?

The first requirement of distributive justice is a shared economic, social, and cultural infrastructure, a public sector that both enlarges the scope of and gives some determinate shape to our private lives: roads, bridges, mass transit, national parks, communication systems, schools, museums, and so on. It may be that the great age of construction in these areas lies behind us; certainly we have lost our sense of the necessary collective base of our everyday social life and of the political decisions and economic costs required to sustain that base. At the moment we are not sustaining it; we stand and watch its slow decay. In itself, I suppose, the decay of the infrastructure is a matter not of justice or injustice but rather of wisdom and foolishness—though contemporary foolishness imposes costs on future generations, and that may be an unjust imposition. Among ourselves, at any rate, we have every right to choose public impoverishment for the sake of private affluence, so long as the choice reflects a democratic decision and so long as the impoverishment and the affluence are shared across the society. But these conditions are rarely met.

The purpose of the infrastructure is to enable the mass of citizens to participate in necessary or valued social activities. Hence its construction and repair, when they are decided upon in some more or less democratic fashion, provide a rough index of contemporary understandings of those activities. Again and again, over long periods of time, money must be appropriated and costs distributed. Should we, to take an easy and obvious example, subsidize the highways and the suburbs or the subways and the cities? How much are we prepared to invest in safety? in recreation? in high culture? These decisions give concrete shape to a way of life. The decay of the infrastructure and its replacement by private facilities has the effect of disabling or excluding some citizens, but not others, from participating in that way of life. Or it has the effect of undercutting the democratic process by which our common ways are shaped.

Let me illustrate that last effect by considering a proposal put forward by the president of a California research institute in the wake of the collapse of a bridge in Connecticut. (The locations of the institute and the bridge are not without significance.) It would be better, the institute president tells us, to sell our highways and bridges "to private firms that would operate them as competing, self-financed business ventures." Travel would then be safer than it is today because "the prospect of a multi-million dollar liability in the event of a bridge collapse would lead the new owners to make rapid, major investments in rebuilding."[1] This is an interesting argument—though not, as it pretends to be, a laissez-faire argument. The safety record of private enterprise has never been very good except when safety is imposed by the state, and so it would be under this proposal, in the form of "multi-million dollar liability." In effect, the proposal to sell highways and bridges to private companies is a proposal to rely on the courts rather than the legislature to set safety standards and user costs.[2] Government is still crucial, but now the least democratic rather than the most democratic branch of government would play the decisive role. If the standards were set very high, the price of maintenance and insurance would be passed on to the men and women who used the roads; if it became impossible to meet those standards and still maintain a respectable profit margin, the "new owners" would quickly apply to the state for a subsidy. Then, indeed, the legislature would have to make a decision, but it would decide under severe (and by now familiar) constraints—for aren't these owners providing essential services? At the same time, whatever profits

1. Robert Poole, "How Should We Fix I-95's Ailing Bridges? By Selling Them Off," *New York Times*, July 9, 1983, op ed page.

2. Robert Nozick provides a full-scale philosophic defense of this position in *Anarchy, State, and Utopia* (New York: Basic Books, 1974), chap. 4.

were made would be invested at the sole discretion of the owners. How, then, would we decide what new roads and bridges to build? It is false to assume that these are merely market decisions; they determine patterns of development, habitation, and work as well as patterns of travel and recreation. And they affect the lives of people whom the owners don't know and will never consult. Nor will the courts consult these people, for though judicial decisions on liability will, at least initially, determine the whole pattern of costs, they will do so with reference only to the entitlements of particular individuals. Even if we assume that justice is done to these individuals, the subsequent shaping of the infrastructure would be unjust to all the rest of us.

The injustice in this case would be political, a failure of democracy (in a country explicitly committed to democratic politics). But this sort of failure may well lead to injustices of another sort. When we decide to subsidize subways, for example, we do so because we want to live in a city of a certain kind, where movement is easy and cultural facilities are generally available, and where individuals are not trapped in their neighborhoods. If such a vision is widely shared, then the decay of the subway system (through public inadvertence) or the lapse of the subsidy (through privatization) is likely to make full participation in the urban economy and culture impossible for some people, who will then plausibly claim that they are being treated unjustly. One can imagine a city, divided, say, into ethnic "quarters," each with its own internal life, where the absence or failure of public transportation would merely confirm the shared understanding of urbanity and injure no one. But we don't live in cities of that sort, and among ourselves the injury would be palpable. Indeed, I can leave the conditional mood behind: the injury is palpable. In an inegalitarian society, the decay of the infrastructure has differential effects, constraining the activities, limiting the scope of some people and not others. These constraints have never been ratified democratically, and they are, in any case, inconsistent with a democratic social life.

The second requirement of distributive justice is a system of communal provision. The infrastructure is enabling, but not everyone is able, and we need to care for the ill, the aged, the infirm, the destitute, the unemployed, and so on. The state has to be a welfare state. This is, I think, a general truth about all states, a moral fact. Every state that I have ever encountered in the study of history and comparative politics is in some sense committed, or at least claims to be committed, to the welfare of its own people (though not necessarily of conquered or captive peoples). Its officials secure the trade routes and the grain supply, organize the irrigation of the fields, appease the gods, ward off hostile foreigners, look after public health, care for widows and orphans, and so on. Or they bustle about importantly pretending to do these things. And these are the sorts of things they ought to do. What in particular they ought to do will depend on the local political culture and the shared understanding of social life. The emphasis of our own welfare state, for example, is overwhelmingly on physical well-being and long life. The amount of money that we spend on health care is probably without precedent in the history of human civilization. That emphasis isn't simply a matter of justice; it would not be unjust, for example, if we spent more of our money on housing, or schooling, or even on science and the arts. Given the prevailing emphasis, however, justice requires that the protection we provide be provided across the class of citizens, to everyone who is ill. I have argued elsewhere that this requires in turn something like a national health service and the enlistment or conscription of physicians for the sake of that service.[3] I won't repeat that argument here; the important claim is simply that the state should respond to the socially recognized needs of its members. That is what the state is for.

The response can take different forms. "A system of communal provision" doesn't necessarily mean a single centralized and uniform system. The requirements of justice are not exact. They do not derive from a doctrine of individual rights such that every individual is entitled, given similar illnesses, say, to exactly the same treatment. If that were the case, then every hospital would have to be organized in the same way, with the same equipment and the same medical procedures. Local differences would be ruled out, even if they were shaped by democratic decisions about budgets, bond issues, hospital government, and so on. Similarly, every schoolchild would have to attend the same sort of school, similarly furnished and equipped, and work through the same curriculum under the guidance of similarly trained teachers and along with an identical mix of other children. None of this is necessary, for

3. Michael Walzer, *Spheres of Justice: A Defense of Pluralism and Equality* (New York: Basic Books, 1983), chap. 3.

the rights in question are social rights; they have their origin in a shared social life, and they partake of the rough and ready character of that life. We make a great mistake when we acquiesce in descriptions of the welfare state as a kind of war against the inevitable and ultimately comfortable messiness of human society: a systematic effort to turn society into "a clean, well-lighted place." No doubt our hospitals should be clean and our urban streets well lit. But there is plenty of room in a welfare state that meets the requirements of justice for chance and risk, for local and diverse arrangements, for voluntary as well as coercive organization, for amateur warmth alongside professional coolness.

The contemporary right-wing demand that government "get off our backs" is entirely legitimate whenever governmental agents interfere with ethnic or religious or regional efforts at collective self-help. But the demand isn't legitimate when it represents (as it most often does) an effort to evade the responsibilities of the collective. This evasion is often masked as a defense of voluntarism and pluralism, but it is also justified, sometimes, in a more direct and forthright way. The responsibilities of the collective have become too onerous, it is said; the costs of the welfare state are too high; and, after all, private life and even private affluence are also central values of American culture. I shall leave aside the standard liberal-left response to this sort of thing, though it is an important and largely true response, namely, that we already run our welfare state on the cheap and that levels of taxation and expenditure are relatively low compared with those of other Western countries. It may be the case that communal sentiment and practical solidarity are so attenuated in American society as to make it difficult to justify higher levels of taxation. But if the costs of welfare are too high in the United States today, then they have to be cut in ways that respect the equal standing of citizens. It is obviously unjust to reduce communal provision only for politically vulnerable men and women and children—so obviously unjust that government officials who do so are compelled to lie about what they are doing.

A more general reduction—not only in funds targeted to desperate individuals and depressed areas but also in medicare, unemployment insurance, and social security—would never command popular support. Is this because we have created a dependent population, men and women with their hands held out, unwilling, perhaps unable, to stand on their own?[4] The description is both condescending and false. We would do better to say that, after long political struggles, the mass of citizens have come to understand the democratic state as a cooperative enterprise and to assert their claim to the fruits of that enterprise. It is not the purpose of the democratic state, rightly understood, to uphold the power of the few or to redistribute wealth to the wealthy—though this is what states have commonly done: the rich have always had their hands out— but to sustain equally the lives and minimal well-being of all its citizens. Even if we were to fall on collective hard times, even if the people were to decide on a lower level of communal provision, this purpose would remain paramount. Hence reductions would have to begin, so to speak, at the top, and they would have to be carried out in ways that did not weaken the position of the weakest citizens. This is a version of Rawls's difference principle that commands not only hypothetical but actual consent. It is expressed in the idea of a "safety net," and were this idea taken seriously, it would probably rule out any reductions at all in current welfare standards: for those reductions that are morally possible are politically impossible, and those that are politically possible are morally barred.

The idea of the "safety net" is a more powerful idea than is commonly thought. It means that the first commitment of the welfare state is to its weakest members; nothing else can be done until their position is secured. What counts as security is a matter for political debate: how high do we hang the net? But answers to this question are not arbitrary; security is a relative term, which has to be understood together with the values of the society and the common expectations of its members. The better-off members are entitled to protect their private lives—as they will anyway be inclined to do in a liberal society—but only so long as they recognize the extent to which those lives are themselves protected by the community as a whole and only so long as they are prepared to extend communal protection to all the other members. In the United States today that extension would require a considerable restructuring of the welfare state for the sake of equal protection. Whether it would also require a refinancing of the welfare state is a question I can leave aside. I suspect that restructuring would entail, for reasons

4. This is a common charge against the welfare state; see, for example, George Gilder, *Wealth and Poverty* (New York: Basic Books, 1981), especially pt. 2.

of political if not moral logic, greater expenditure, but if we were prepared to spend less money enhancing the lives of the rich and the merely prosperous, we could probably spend less money simply. The crucial point is that the safety net be constructed so as to secure for everyone whatever it is we collectively believe to be the central values of our culture, the needs that must be met if we are to stand to one another as *fellow* citizens.

The third requirement of distributive justice is nicely stated in the classical liberal slogan about "equality of opportunity." But this slogan is not well understood when it is taken to legitimize the familiar forms of competition—as if the goals of the competitive race are given, and only the number and the handicaps of the runners are at issue. In fact, the three words "equality of opportunity" tell us nothing about what opportunities ought to be available. It's not the case that opportunities are fixed forever in the prevailing set; nor are they necessarily responsive, even in a liberal society, to individual preference. We need not set about opening career paths to feudal lordship or political tyranny, for example, even if there are people around who long to be lords and tyrants. We discourage such ambitions, forcibly if necessary; and the discouragement is in no sense unjust. Nor would it be unjust if we were to discourage ambitions for the higher forms of capitalist ownership. We tell ambitious bureaucrats that they can climb the institutional ladder only so far: unlimited power is not within their reach. Similarly, we might tell ambitious entrepreneurs that they can enrich themselves only so far: unlimited wealth (ownership of the major means of production, say) is not within their reach. What the range of opportunities should be is something, again, that can only be decided politically and that always has to be decided with reference to a particular set of cultural values and social understandings.

In the United States today, there are three social goods to which equality of opportunity is relevant: the first is office (in both bureaucracies and the professions); the second is money or market power; the third is political power. With regard to all three, strong anti-authoritarian tendencies are at work, and have been at work for some time, reflecting the deepest values of a liberal and democratic culture. We can think of these tendencies as imposing limits on available opportunities. Review boards, consent requirements, collective bargaining, grievance procedures, government licensing of radio and television stations, democratic politics itself—all these instrumentalities restrict what one can do with office, wealth, and power. Conceivably, these restrictions make the goods less *good*, less attractive to the men and women who seek or hold them; certainly, the restrictions make the goods less dangerous to the men and women who don't seek or hold them. In any case, the nature of the competition changes as the nature of the opportunities change. It is easier to succeed and less disastrous to fail when goods are limited (not in number but) in value. Equality of opportunity is more likely when the slope of ambition and advantage is less steep.

This rule holds for two reasons. First, unlimited office, wealth, and power make it possible for those who win such goods to close off opportunities to everyone else. Indeed, the failure of limits in any one sphere endangers equality of opportunity in all the others—for unlimited wealth can buy office and power, unlimited power can control the market and shape the professions, and so on. This is the common historical pattern, and it explains most of the standard inequalities. Today's inequalities of opportunity derive from yesterday's victories and defeats; they are inherited from the past, carried not by genetic but by social structures, by organized power, wealth, and professional standing. But the rule holds for a second reason also. When we open old opportunities to new groups of competitors, the immediate effect is to intensify the competition, to generate the classical rat race. And the rat race is not an ideal setting for equality of opportunity. One might say that the rat race provides opportunities only for rats. An exaggeration, perhaps, but the statement is not wholly untrue. When competition is too fierce (because the stakes are too high), all sorts of social and psychological mechanisms come into play to foster aggressive and ruthless behavior among some people and withdrawal and resignation among others. To some extent, the resulting pattern will overlap with older patterns of class or group subordination; to some extent, its shape will be new. But if we imagine equality of opportunity as it was conventionally imagined among liberals and democrats, as a way of creating an open, fluid, and lively social life, the rat race represents a defeat. There isn't, so to speak, enough room on the steep slope of ambition and advantage.

Equality of opportunity won't work unless the slope is flattened— and that is what the democratic understanding of office, wealth, and power also requires. Hence it is what justice requires. It must still be possible, in a society like ours, to exercise professional authority, make money in the marketplace, win political power. These are legitimate opportunities—so long as they are available only in ways that don't establish positions of privilege, social strongholds that other men and women can take only by storm and that are always desperately defended. Since many opportunities are both attractive and exclusive, competition is inevitable, and so is winning and losing; nor will winning ever lose its sweetness or losing its bitterness. But it is possible to describe a society—different from but also deriving from our own society—in which winning doesn't breed arrogance and domination and losing doesn't breed servility and subjection, and in which winners and losers can imagine themselves in each other's places. This is, after all, the actual experience of democratic politics. Powerful men and women lose elections and surrender their power. They must be ready to do that and then to return to private life, for otherwise opposition would be too dangerous and the right of opposition never fully established or widely exercised. Similarly, equality of opportunity requires a (relatively) easy mobility up and down the scale of professional and financial standing. That mobility is not easily established, either for individuals or for families, but its acceptance is more likely if the advantages that go with office and money are less far-reaching than they are today.

If we are committed to equal opportunity, then, we would do best to reduce the steepness of the slope of advantage. This is not the goal that is served by contemporary affirmative action programs; they aim instead at making the existing scramble for office and money more accessible to women and to minority groups and, by virtue of that new accessibility, more fair. The scramble should be more fair; such programs, so long as they avoid rigid quotas, are readily defensible. I would argue, however, that they will have only a limited and local effect if the men and women they advance merely take over established positions. The point is to change the nature of the positions, and so offer to the men and women who come next the prospect of a scramble that is at once more lively and less fierce, for a wider range of opportunities.

The fourth requirement of distributive justice is a strong democracy. In a sense, equality of opportunity encompasses the argument for democracy because it requires that political power be widely available to

[*145*]

citizens. This requirement is important for two reasons: first, because power is a good thing to have (it is even a good thing to share, that is, to have in something less than the strongest sense of the word "have"); second, because power is the crucial instrument for determining infrastructural and welfare state priorities and for shaping available opportunities in other fields. It has intrinsic and instrumental value, and the experience of these values should be common and readily accessible in a democratic society.

Justice, however, requires not only the openness of the sphere of power but also its integrity. Wherever the exercise of power takes on political forms, wherever it is sustained, serious, and extensive, it must be subject to the distributional rules of democratic politics. For now I shall simply assume the existence and importance of these rules—free speech, free assembly, periodic elections, and so on. The question I want to raise has to do with the area over which they are enforced. In a capitalist society, historically, enforcement is barred from the marketplace; entrepreneurs and property owners are exempt from the requirements of democracy; a line is drawn between economy and polity. The establishment of unions and collective bargaining under the sponsorship or at least the protection of the state blurs that line. So does the steady growth of governmental regulation. It is time now to think about the reasons for unions and for regulations and to attempt a more explicit and radical boundary revision.

The reasons have to do with what goes on in the economic sphere. If we focus narrowly on entrepreneurial activity and on petty-bourgeois enterprise, we can, perhaps, describe a "pure" economy: all transactions, or by far the greater number of transactions, can plausibly be talked about in the language of free exchange. But if we focus on the modern corporation, all such plausibility vanishes. For corporations are—this is now a commonplace of American political science—private governments; their transactions are significantly political in character, taking the form of command and obedience rather than free exchange; their owners and agents make decisions that determine the costs and the risks that other people must live with.[5] It is the experience of private government that prompts the internal opposition of unions and the

5. There is a large literature on private government; for a recent and especially useful discussion, see Charles E. Lindblom, *Politics and Markets* (New York: Basic Books, 1977), chaps. 13 and 14.

external interventions of the state. The unions represent men and women directly subject to corporate power; the state represents men and women radically affected by corporate decisions. But these two forms of representation are only sometimes effective, and effective then only to a limited degree, because corporate power at its core remains exempt from the rules of democracy. The exemption is defended, these days, not with an argument that private government is after all legitimate, but with a denial that private government exists: there is no one out here but us entrepreneurs. Since the denial is false, justice requires that we challenge the exemption and explore systematically the alternatives to private government: public ownership and workers' control and various combinations of the two.

Marxists have long argued that the fundamental moral problem of the capitalist economy (if there is a *moral* problem at all) is exploitation, not domination, the extraction of surplus value through the productive process, not the tyrannical control of production.[6] The theory of exploitation, at least as it has commonly been understood, makes a strong claim: that workers are literally robbed of value that they and only they create. They work but don't reap the full benefits of their work; someone else benefits who hasn't worked at all. The injustice is plain, at least if one accepts Marx's account of the creation of value. Conceivably, the injustice would still be plain even if one recognized a wider creativity than Marx allows for: it might still be said that workers don't get their "fair share" of the surplus they help to create. That, indeed, is what workers commonly say when they demand higher wages. But the complaint about *unfair shares* isn't the most important of their complaints. For exploitation is merely one consequence of the failure of democracy in economic life. When wages are very low, it looks like the crucial consequence and the necessary focus of working-class militancy. It isn't, however, an issue that can be addressed by itself. Private government is a prior issue—not only in theory: it always, in fact, comes first. The earliest and sharpest form of class struggle is the struggle against the tyranny of owners and foremen, the daily discipline

---

6. Robert Tucker argues for the centrality of the idea of domination, in the economy as well as the state, in *The Marxian Revolutionary Idea* (New York: Norton, 1969). Marxist views of justice have been much debated in recent years; for some of the best statements, see Marshall Cohen, Thomas Nagel, and Thomas Scanlon, eds., *Marx, Justice, and History* (Princeton: Princeton University Press, 1980).

of the workplace, the arbitrary layoffs and firings; and the earliest and greatest working-class victories are the victories that bring union recognition, grievance procedures, seniority rules, and so on. It is the distribution of power, not of surplus value, that is crucial. Power is instrumental to the acquisition of surplus value, but that is never the only reason for seeking it; citizenship and self-respect are also at stake.

As a political economist, not a moralist, Marx argued that capitalism had created vast collective enterprises that would necessarily come under collective control. I don't know if that argument is right; I'm not a political economist. But the argument has a moral analogue, in which "should" substitutes for "would"—and the analogue is certainly right. Collective enterprises should be governed collectively, in accordance with the shared understanding of how such government works. Among ourselves, that understanding is democratic: hence, again, the requirement of industrial democracy.

Industrial democracy will make for "fair shares," but only in this special sense: that some particular idea of fairness will be chosen over some other idea, and the idea that is chosen will command widespread support. There are, indeed, many claims on surplus value—entrepreneurial profits and capital costs; investment; the social costs of welfare, safety, environmental protection; management costs; research costs; worker shares, which can be paid in money or in time; and so on— and many different proposals for an equitable or a prudent division. Though market considerations are relevant to all these claims, we must also make political choices. The theory of exploitation does not help us much to make these choices, for there is no division of surplus value, so much here, so much there, that is just in itself. But a division that is the work of democratic citizens will at least reflect current understandings of justice, and it will leave the way open for better understandings.

Throughout this paper I have emphasized the importance of politics. The social infrastructure, the pattern of communal provision, the range of opportunities, the division of surplus value: all these must be decided politically, though always with reference to shared understandings that are themselves worked out through deeper social processes. Hence political justice, or democracy, is the immediate form of justice. But democracy, though it rests ultimately upon a substantive distribution

of power—one citizen, one vote—takes in practice the form of a pro-
cedural allocation of power—chiefly through free elections. And elections have unpredictable outcomes; the resulting distributive decisions
are, sometimes, unjust. So justice requires that justice itself be democratically at risk. This means that your favored conception, or mine,
of infrastructural priorities, or the necessary forms of welfare, or the
nature of available opportunities, or the division of this or that factory's
profits, may be rejected. Justice is not likely to be achieved by the
enactment of a single philosophy of justice, but rather of this philosophical view and then of that one, insofar as these views seem to the
citizens to capture the moral realities of their common life. And the
enactment is always, as I said at the beginning,"in confusion"—justice
is not an instant and exact order; it isn't the end of political contention.

The contention is endless, but it isn't philosophically uncontrolled.
Political argument is not a matter of searching randomly for whatever
claims, examples, or precedents will help us on our way to victory; it
is not a matter of rhetorical gesture or mere expedience. Individuals
and groups will, of course, defend their particular interests as best they
can, but they must also refer themselves to the common interests and
the shared values of their society. They are participants in a process
not only of egoistic assertion but also of collective interpretation. In
the United States today, that process has its beginning in an account
of the meaning of citizenship. I have been assuming such an account,
and it has provided me with an egalitarian baseline: for citizenship in
a democratic state entails equality. But citizenship doesn't reproduce
equality in all the spheres of social life—not even in politics itself,
where the allocation of power through elections makes some citizens
more powerful than others. How much equality is appropriate to each
sphere is a difficult question, for it depends on interpretations that lack
certainty and on decisions that lack finality. We can get things wrong.
Indeed, it has been my claim in this essay that we have gotten things
wrong and made our citizens more unequal than they ought to be. We
have not sustained the infrastructure that our social life requires. We
have not made a sufficient commitment to communal provision. We
have not provided a wide enough range of opportunities. We have not
challenged the power of private governments. Justice requires that we
do all these things, but it also requires that we do them democratically.
Hence the burden that egalitarian philosophers must accept: to provide

a persuasive interpretation of democratic citizenship and then of the goods and opportunities that citizens distribute to one another—I mean American citizens, here and now, who rightly have the authoritative (but never the final) word.

[7]

Equally Endowed with Rights

WALTER BERNS

I address this subject from the perspective of American constitutional law, not as a philosopher or even as a political theorist. Yet, contrary to what is implied by the internal organization of our universities, constitutional law and philosophy or political theory are not isolated one from another, and emphatically not in the United States. The law in question derives from a constitution that is related to the Declaration of Independence as effect is related to cause, and the Declaration of Independence, the cause, is a political statement of a philosophical teaching concerning the nature of man, Providence, and nature itself. In it we learn that nature's God endows all men with the rights of life, liberty, and the pursuit of happiness, and that government is instituted to secure these rights. That the Constitution was understood by its framers to have as its purpose the establishment of such a government there can be little doubt.[1] Thus, if he is to do his job properly, the

1. *Federalist* 84; Richard Henry Lee to George Mason, October 1, 1787, in Robert A. Rutland, ed., *The Papers of George Mason* (Chapel Hill: University of North Carolina Press, 1970), 3: 997–98; James Wilson, State House Speech, October 6, 1787, in John Bach McMaster and Frederick D. Stone, eds., *Pennsylvania and the Federal Constitution, 1787–1788* (Lancaster: Historical Society of Pennsylvania, 1888), pp. 143–44; "Letters from the Federal Farmer," no. 4, October 12, 1787, in Herbert J. Storing, ed., *The Complete Anti-Federalist* (Chicago: University of Chicago Press, 1981), 2: 247–49.

professor of constitutional law must be thoroughly familiar with the political philosophy that informs the Constitution.

This judgment of how to profess constitutional law is not widely shared today, however, and is explicitly denied by the most prominent of contemporary legal philosophers, Ronald Dworkin. In his influential book, *Taking Rights Seriously*, Dworkin recognizes that there can be no constitutional law independent of philosophy, but he maintains that until recently there has been no philosophy—or, at least, no *good* philosophy—to which constitutional law can be attached. "Constitutional law can make no genuine advance until it isolates the problem of rights against the state and makes that problem part of its own agenda. That argues for a fusion of constitutional law and moral theory, a connection that, incredibly, has yet to take place."[2] In saying this, Dworkin suggests that the existence of the "state" can be taken for granted and therefore that the task for legal philosophers is the development of a "theory of moral rights against [it]." The Framers, to the contrary, took the rights for granted and understood their task to be that of building a "state" in order to secure them. This was their way of taking rights seriously.

The necessity of a "state," or, to employ the Framers' term, of government, is a consequence of the nature of human beings and the rights they naturally possess. All persons are created equal insofar as they are equally endowed with the rights to life, liberty, and the pursuit of a self-defined happiness. These, the Framers proclaimed, were self-evident truths. People are not, however, by nature equally angelic; if they were, as James Madison pointed out in *Federalist* 51, government would be unnecessary and constitutional limitations on government would be supererogatory. On the contrary, as the Framers learned from the natural right philosophers, in their natural condition people are selfish, concerned primarily with preserving themselves, and—there being no government and, indeed, no rules against their doing so— equally free to adopt any means to preserve themselves. They have a right to do so, and, because they exercise this right, their natural condition is one of war (of every person against every other), and their life is "solitary, poor, nasty, brutish, and short." This famous for-

2. Ronald Dworkin, *Taking Rights Seriously* (Cambridge: Harvard University Press, 1977), p. 149.

mulation is, of course, Thomas Hobbes's,[3] the first political philosopher to take rights seriously—insofar as he was the first to describe them and to take his bearings from them—and the first of the modern egalitarians. What was needed was peace, and, happily, people are equally endowed with passions that incline them to peace: their fear of death, their desire for such things as are necessary to commodious living, "and a hope by their industry to obtain them."[4] Unlike other animals (who are governed by their instincts), humans are also endowed with reason: "And reason suggesteth articles of peace, upon which men may be drawn to agreement." Hobbes calls these articles the laws of nature, which direct us to exchange our natural rights for the peace that only government can provide.[5] Only a government with powers over us can provide peace among us.

On the basis of a somewhat similar judgment of our nature, John Locke (sometimes referred to as "America's philosopher") made a similar analysis. "To avoid this state of war," he said, "is one great reason of men's putting themselves in society and quitting the state of nature."[6] The rights are possessed in nature but only insecurely. Hence, as the Declaration of Independence restates the teaching, "to secure these rights, governments are instituted among men." When instituting such a government, or, as Madison put it in *Federalist* 51, in framing it, "the great difficulty lies in this: you must first enable the government to control the governed; and in the next place oblige it to control itself." Precisely because they took rights seriously, and had no illusions about the inclinations of the men who were endowed with these rights, the Framers instituted a government with powers (legislative, executive, and judicial); they did so in a Constitution that did not contain a formal bill of rights or (except in Article I, sec. 8, where the word appears in a clause empowering Congress "to promote the progress of science and useful arts") even mention the word "rights" (or "a right"). In their defense, Alexander Hamilton insisted that "the Constitution is itself, in every rational sense, and to every useful purpose, A BILL OF RIGHTS."[7]

3. Thomas Hobbes, *Leviathan*, chap. 13.
4. Ibid.
5. Ibid., chap. 14.
6. John Locke, *Treatises* II, sec. 21.
7. *Federalist* 84.

If in the state of nature every man is absolute lord of his own person (Locke's formulation), "equal to the greatest, and subject to nobody," then no man, unless he give his consent, may rightfully be governed by another. The Constitution is an expression of that consent and, in that sense, is an exercise of the natural right to govern oneself and to specify the terms according to which one agrees to be governed by others. In this respect, the Constitution is a bill of natural rights.

It is also a bill of civil rights insofar as its structure, or the way it organizes the powers it vests in government, is designed to secure or protect civil rights. To this end, a well-designed structure is likely to prove more efficacious than a formal statement of rights against government. Historically, Hamilton argued, bills of rights have been "stipulations between kings and their subjects, abridgements of prerogative in favor of privilege," and their terms have been enforced, if at all, by the political power brought to bear by parliaments. But in the United States there would be no king, and there would be no subjects with privileges; there would only be citizens, acting in the name of all and exercising the power of all. That power was to be feared. After all, those citizens, at least as they make up the American civil society, have all the power of Hobbes's sovereign, who, we need to remind ourselves, was authorized (or brought into being) in order to secure rights. It was to him that the contracting parties yielded their rights to govern themselves. True, in Locke's version, followed by the Framers, the contracting parties yielded their rights not to a Hobbesian sovereign but to a lawmaking authority, because there would be greater safety when the sovereign was authorized to act only through the law or by means of law.[8] This was so if only because everyone, even those who joined in the making of it, would be subject to law. Still, how much safety would there be if the lawmaking power were put in the hands of a simple majority of citizens? The Framers feared such a majority would be a faction, by which they meant a majority "actuated by some common impulse of passion, or of interest, adverse to the rights of other citizens, or to the permanent and aggregate interests of the community."[9] Against such a majority a bill of rights would provide little protection. For instance, were the so-called Moral Majority really a majority and al-

8. Locke, *Treatises* II, secs. 22, 87, 89, 136, 138.
9. *Federalist* 10.

lowed to exercise the legislative power of the people of the United States, it would not be likely to respect the rights of (what is by implication) the immoral minority. Indeed, if, even under the Constitution, the Moral Majority were to become a *political* majority, it would be unlikely to accept the restraints imposed on it by the judiciary. On the contrary, it would be likely to strip the judiciary of its powers, deprive it of its jurisdiction in cases involving school prayers, for example, or abortion. Rights can be secured only when government by majority factions is prevented, and this can be accomplished—and, on the whole, has been accomplished—by preventing the political formation of majority factions. The precise means of accomplishing this end were the institutional arrangements Madison called "auxiliary precautions."[10] Their purpose was, and is, to achieve government by constitutional majorities—majorities assembled from representatives of the people—rather than by popular majorities, which is to say majorities assembled directly from the people. After all, the purpose of government is to secure the equal rights of all, not to foster the greatest good for the greatest number. The Constitution, with the powers it vests in government as well as its complex organization of those powers, is the consequence of taking rights seriously.

The fundamental soundness of this constitutional plan has been demonstrated in and by our history, and nowhere more dramatically than on the principal occasion when it failed. During the Civil War, when the division on the slavery issue threatened permanently to divide the country, all sorts of rights were denied: newspapers were shut down, persons were held in jail without being brought to trial, and, for one more example, civilians were tried by military courts. This failure and some others derive from a systemic failure at the beginning: the denial to most black people of the fundamental natural right not to be governed without their consent. Most of them had no opportunity to vote for or against the ratification of the Constitution. It was therefore almost inevitable that they would be denied the rights enjoyed by other Americans, and, most important, the right to be represented in constitutional majorities. The consequence—one of many—was that they remained slaves, and, as time passed, what was required to keep them slaves was the formation of a single-interest political party and the onset of

10. *Federalist* 51.

single-issue politics, leading to what came close to being a permanent division of the country. Madison spoke to this point when he said, in *Federalist* 51, that in a free government "the security for civil rights must be the same as that for religious rights. It consists in the one case in the multiplicity of interests, and in the other in the multiplicity of [religious] sects." The object was to avoid divisions in which majority and minority were divided on a single issue, especially a moral issue; and slavery was a moral issue.

It was a moral issue for which the Framers had no policy other than the ill-founded hope that if slavery were confined to the states where it then existed,[11] it would eventually cease to be profitable, at which time emancipation (or at least manumission) would become possible— if it could be combined with colonization. They knew slavery was contrary to natural right,[12] but there is little evidence that they expected the bulk of the black population to be incorporated into "the people of the United States." On the contrary: "nothing is more certainly written in the book of fate," Jefferson wrote in his autobiography, "than that these people are to be free; nor is it less certain that the two races, equally free, cannot live in the same government."[13] But why not? Since blacks were the equals of whites with respect to natural rights, why should they not join whites as citizens of the United States (or, in the context of Jefferson's answer, of Virginia)? "Deep-rooted prejudices entertained by the whites; ten thousand recollections, by the blacks, of the injuries they have sustained; new provocations; the real distinctions which nature has made; and many other circumstances, will divide us into parties, and produce convulsions, which will probably never end but in the extermination of the one or the other race."[14] Jefferson was not alone in this judgment or in the conclusion he drew from it: colonization was the only safe policy. A constitution founded

11. See Walter Berns, "The Constitution and the Migration of Slaves," *Yale Law Journal* 78 (December 1968): 198–228.

12. See Thomas Jefferson, *Notes on the State of Virginia*, Query XVIII, and, e.g., the remarks of James Madison, Gouverneur Morris, and Luther Martin in Max Farrand, ed., *The Records of the Federal Convention of 1787* (New Haven: Yale University Press, 1937), 1: 135, 588; 2: 364.

13. Thomas Jefferson, "Autobiography," in Adrienne Koch and William Peden, eds., *The Life and Selected Writings of Thomas Jefferson* (New York: Modern Library, 1944), p. 51.

14. Jefferson, *Notes on the State of Virginia*, Query XIV.

on the principle that all persons are equal in their possession of natural rights would nevertheless have to acknowledge that they are unequal in other respects. And race was not the only respect in which people were unequal; they also were endowed with "different and unequal faculties."

Continuing the process of Locke's reformulation of Hobbes, the Framers translated the right of self-preservation into its constituent parts of life, liberty, and—not estate, but—happiness, and not happiness as such but rather its pursuit. Some might say that individuals are equally entitled to happiness, but the government charged with the duty to secure a right to happiness would have to know what happiness is, and the Framers made no such claim. On the contrary, they seem to have taken it as settled by Hobbes and Locke that not only did human beings not share a common *opinion* of happiness or of the good life, but *knowledge* of happiness or of the good life was unobtainable, beyond the reach of the profoundest minds. Like Hobbes and Locke, again, they accepted the consequences that flowed from this understanding. Rather than putting its power or the weight of its influence behind a particular view of happiness—or a particular church, for example—the government they instituted would protect the right of everyone to go his own way, to lead an essentially private life. Individuals have "different and unequal faculties" for pursuing happiness, which means they will define it differently and in its pursuit succeed unequally, but there is no way, consistent with natural right, that government can guarantee equal success.

Individuals also have "different and unequal faculties" for acquiring property, which many of them regard as a condition of happiness, and the Framers' government will respect those inequalities as it protects the equal rights. In fact, because they had been educated by Adam Smith and his precursor, John Locke, the Framers understood the special significance of securing the property right. With that security would come economic prosperity, which they saw as a condition of free government. Consequently, they were determined to create an atmosphere congenial to the improvement of "arts, manufactures, and commerce" (Smith's phrase),[15] which they accomplished, in part, by securing

15. Adam Smith, *The Wealth of Nations*, bk. V, chap. 1, pt. III, art. 3 ("Of the Expence of the Institutions for the Instruction of People of All Ages"), Modern Library ed., p. 755.

to authors and inventors "the exclusive right to their respective writings and discoveries." Americans were to be tied to economic progress by a constitutional right. The Framers—here in the person of James Madison—went so far as to assert that the first object of government is "the protection of different and unequal faculties of acquiring property."[16] From that protection would come, and did come, not only different "kinds" of property but "different degrees" of property. Wealth would be unequally distributed.

Yet Madison's statement is wholly in accord with the original natural rights teaching. The only respect in which individuals are equal is in the possession of the rights nature endows them with; they are not equally endowed with those faculties—intelligence, energy, pertinacity, inventiveness, or whatever—in which, as Madison says, "the rights of property originate." To secure the rights of all persons is to secure the rights of otherwise unequally endowed persons, and thereby to ensure that some will become rich and others will not. But to do so also ensures economic development. For to protect the faculties of acquiring property, even if—or especially if—those faculties are possessed unequally, is to promote the creation of wealth; it is to give vent to those faculties and to the acquisitive spirit. By assuring the more enterprising that they may earn all they can and keep much of what they rightfully earn, society stands to profit from their enterprise. In fact, it inspires almost everyone to become enterprising. Hamilton put it this way in *Federalist* 12:

> The prosperity of commerce is now perceived and acknowledged by all enlightened statesmen to be the most useful as well as the most productive source of national wealth, and has accordingly become a primary object of their political cares. By multiplying the means of gratification, by promoting the introduction and circulation of the precious metals, those darling objects of human avarice and enterprise, it serves to vivify and invigorate all the channels of industry and to make them flow with greater activity and copiousness. The assiduous merchant, the laborious husbandman, the active mechanic, and the industrious manufacturer—all orders of men look forward with eager expectation and growing alacrity to this pleasing reward of their toils.

16. *Federalist* 10.

Without attempting to elucidate every aspect of the Framers' plan, I would characterize it as follows: Unlike the political economies under which nations had been governed in the past, the American economy would not be governed by scarcity. There would be more than enough to go around. The wealth of this nation would grow a thousandfold and more, as Locke had promised,[17] and while the wealth would be unequally distributed, our rich (unlike the feudal rich) would have no interest in keeping the poor down, and our poor (unlike the feudal poor) would have no interest in bringing the rich down.

The exception to this plan, like the exceptions to so many generalizations about America, would be found in the feudal South, and like so many other exceptions, this one proves (or proved) the rule. Tocqueville, upon crossing the river from Ohio to Kentucky, remarked the difference between the two political economies in a letter to his father:

> For the first time we have had a chance to examine there the effect that slavery produces on society. On the right bank of the Ohio everything is activity, industry; labour is honored; there are no slaves. Pass to the left bank and the scene changes so suddenly that you think yourself on the other side of the world; the enterprising spirit is gone. There, work is not only painful, it's shameful, and you degrade yourself in submitting yourself to it. To ride, to hunt, to smoke like a Turk in the sunshine: there is the destiny of the White.[18]

The life of that southern white depended on his being able to keep the blacks down, and to do so he depended on the constitution and laws of his particular state and (except in the matter of fugitive slaves) not on those of the United States. In fact, the Constitution, especially in its original unamended text, is remarkably free of references to groups, genders, or classes, and it bestows no class privileges. Everyone was encouraged to work and expected to gain from it, and, as a consequence, the politics of the nation would be peaceful. This "busyness" was one of the things that struck Tocqueville when he first landed in America. As he wrote his father,

17. Locke, *Treatises* II, secs. 37, 40, 43.
18. George Wilson Pierson, *Tocqueville and Beaumont in America* (New York: Oxford University Press, 1938), p. 582.

Everybody works, and the mine is so rich that all those who work rapidly succeed in acquiring that which renders existence happy. The most active spirits, like the most tranquil, find enough to fill their lives here without busying themselves troubling the state. The restlessness which so wracks our European societies seems to cooperate toward the prosperity of this one.[19]

What I have written to this point can be summarized as follows: The Framers took it for granted that all are equally endowed with rights and that, given human passions and the ways in which we were driven to satisfy them, those rights could not be secured without a government possessed of powers sufficient "to control the governed." They also took it for granted that those rights could not be secured (even under government) if government were not "obliged to control itself." Here they were particularly concerned with what might be done by popular majorities, and properly so because they were creating a popular government. They therefore structured or organized power in such a way that it could not readily be used to deprive the minority of its rights. ("In the extent and proper structure of the Union, therefore, we behold a republican remedy for the diseases most incident to republican [i.e., popular] government.")[20] Chief among these diseases was faction (whose "latent causes [are] sown in the nature of man"),[21] and chief among the causes of faction were "different [and zealous] opinions concerning religion," as well as passionate attachments to "different leaders ambitiously contending for pre-eminence and power; or to persons of other descriptions whose fortunes have been interesting to the human passions."[22] They therefore subordinated religion, removing it from the public to the private sphere, and accentuated property and the right to acquire it. There were to be no American Savonarolas, Cromwells, or Caesars. By emphasizing property and the means of material gratification, the Framers hoped to cause Americans, and especially the "most active spirits" among them, to "fill their lives" not with visions of heaven or glory, and then "troubling the state," but with productive work. If they succeeded in this endeavor, American politics would be

19. Ibid., p. 115. See also p. 119.
20. *Federalist* 10.
21. Ibid.
22. Ibid.

characterized not by an animosity of factions but by a competition of economic interests. Competition of this sort could be peaceful. Unlike that between Protestants and Catholics, Anglicans and Scottish Covenanters, or Caesars and Brutuses, this competition could be regulated by the laws enacted by a popularly elected government. In fact, its regulation "forms the principal task of modern legislation."[23] When properly regulated, the wealth of the nation will increase tremendously. Central to this regulation is protection of the property right.

As the term was used by the Framers, however, property meant more than chattels, land, and buildings. "By property," Locke wrote, "I must be understood . . . to mean that property which men have in their persons as well as goods." While, in his account, individuals surrender their natural freedom and enter into commonwealths chiefly to preserve their property, Locke made it clear that by property he meant "their lives, liberty, and estates."[24]

Madison conveyed this meaning exactly when he wrote that, in its larger sense, property "embraces every thing to which a man may attach a value and have a right; and *which leaves to everyone else a like advantage.*" In a word, he went on, "as a man is said to have a right to his property, he may be equally said to have a property in his rights." And, again like Locke, Madison said government is "instituted to protect property of every sort; as well that which lies in the various rights of individuals, as that which the term particularly expresses."[25]

With all this said, however, it was generally understood at the time that property in the narrow sense occupied a special place in a government intended to secure rights. Not only would protection of the property right lead "all orders of men" to work hard and thereby add to the wealth of the nation, but property was seen as a kind of metaphor serving to remind people of their rights in general and, by doing so, serving to protect them all in practice. The person who can say "This is mine" or "I have a legal right to this" has one of the qualities essential to citizenship in a liberal democracy: the property right is a tangible reminder (and for most people the most effective reminder) of other rights and therefore of the proper limits of government. Those

23. Ibid.
24. Locke, *Treatises* II, secs. 173, 123.
25. Gaillard Hunt, ed., *The Writings of James Madison* (New York, 1906), 6: 101, 102.

limits are defined by our rights. If government can take that which we can feel, taste, smell, and hear, that from which we derive our physical sustenance, why may it not rightly deprive us of other, less tangible goods? For these reasons, then, a "state" that takes rights seriously must secure the rights of property.

There are reasons to find fault with this constitutional system and the life it promotes. The pious Jew has reason to complain of a society that, despite its vaunted toleration, imposes burdens on him who observes a Sabbath different from that of the majority. The devout Christian is justified in concluding that, despite the right of everyone to pursue happiness as he defines it, there seems to be (as there was intended to be) something at work in this liberal democracy that inhibits the truly devout, something that, at a minimum, distracts them from the path described by the saints of the past. Indeed, all who believe that they are commanded above all to love God and their neighbor as they love themselves cannot be indifferent to—cannot be happy with—our policy of indifference toward each other. They will have cause especially to complain of the unequal distribution of wealth and income, even of the absence of any commonly acknowledged moral principle by which we measure the justice of distribution. Protecting the equal rights of unequally endowed persons—to say nothing here of those millions of historically unequally advantaged, or severely disadvantaged, persons—leads to unequal distribution, and not only of wealth. As Ronald Dworkin emphasizes, it also leads to an unequal distribution of "concern and respect," and this, he says, amounts to a denial of the right to "equal concern and respect."

As he sees it, this right is fundamental; he even calls it a "natural right," although, as Thomas Pangle has pointed out, he never attempts to demonstrate that the right is "intrinsic to man as man and not merely part of a deeply-instilled [prejudice] possessed by human beings living in a particular historical epoch."[26] Be that as it may, in Dworkin's view the property right must give way to any social welfare policy required by this "fundamental right of citizens to equal concern and respect."[27] Like many modern egalitarians, Dworkin ends up favoring equality of condition rather than the equality of rights affirmed in the

26. Dworkin, *Taking Rights Seriously*, pp. 176, 182; Thomas Pangle, "Rediscovering Rights," *Public Interest* 50 (Winter 1978): 158–59.

27. Dworkin, *Taking Rights Seriously*, pp. 273, 277, 278, and passim.

Declaration of Independence and embodied in the Constitution. He does so, typically, because, unlike the Framers, he refuses to accept the political and social consequences of recognizing the respects in which people are by nature *un*equal.[28]

The Constitution, the Framers' solution to the political problem identified by the natural rights philosophers, may indeed be an anachronism; surely the ideas that inform it have been under attack from the beginning and even before. (It is sufficient to point to Rousseau.) There is no doubt that the critiques made in the books and by some members of the academy—Dworkin is only the most recent of these—have begun to reverberate in our politics: we hear more and more of group rights or group entitlements, and our politicians speak more and more of compassion. And whatever else might be said about it, the Constitution cannot be described as a compassionate document or to have been conceived in a compassionate spirit: it is too sober for that, too alert to the frailties of human character and the necessity to guard against them. It may secure the rights of man, but the spokesman for our age, Karl Marx, dismissed these as nothing but the rights of bourgeois men.[29]

Yet, compared with its impact elsewhere in the Western world (and beyond), Marxism has few adherents among Americans, not even—in fact, especially—among those intended to be its beneficiaries, the working class. The Constitution might, therefore, survive a while longer and, with the help of the civil rights legislation enacted under its auspices, secure those rights better than ever. The least that can be said for it—and here even some of its critics might agree—is that the available alternatives are unacceptable.

28. Dworkin's account of rights depends on John Rawls, *A Theory of Justice* (Cambridge: Belknap Press of Harvard University Press, 1971). For a critique of Rawls's project and, by implication, of Dworkin's, see Allan Bloom, ''Justice: John Rawls vs. the Tradition of Political Philosophy,'' *American Political Science Review* 69 (June 1975): 648–62.

29. Marx had nothing but contempt for the idea of rights. See his ''On the Jewish Question,'' in Karl Marx and Friedrich Engels, *Collected Works* (New York: International Publishers, 1975), 3: 162.

Suggested Readings

Ackerman, Bruce. *Social Justice in the Liberal State*. New Haven: Yale University Press, 1980. Pt. 2.

Amnesty International of the U.S.A. *Torture in the Eighties*. New York, 1984.

Cohen, Marshall, et al., eds. *Equality and Preferential Treatment*. Princeton: Princeton University Press, 1976.

Epstein, David. *The Political Theory of the Federalist*. Chicago: University of Chicago Press, 1984.

Feinberg, Joel. *Doing and Deserving*. Princeton: Princeton University Press, 1970.

Gilder, George. *Wealth and Poverty*. New York: Basic Books, 1981.

Goldman, Alan. *Justice and Reverse Discrimination*. Princeton: Princeton University Press, 1979.

Goldwin, Robert, and William Schambra. *How Democratic is the Constitution?* Washington, D.C.: American Enterprise Institute for Public Policy Research, 1980.

Hegel, Georg Wilhelm Friedrich. "The State." In *The Philosophy of Right*, translated by T. M. Know. Oxford: Clarendon Press, 1942.

Hildreth, Richard. *Despotism in America*. New York: Kelley, 1970; first published 1854.

Jefferson, Thomas. *The Portable Jefferson*. Edited by Merrill Peterson. New York: Penguin, 1977.

Jensen, Merrill, ed. *Tracts of the American Revolution, 1763–1776*. Indianapolis: Bobbs-Merrill, 1967.

Lindblom, Charles. *Politics and Markets*. New York: Basic Books, 1977.

Madison, James. *The Mind of the Founder*. Edited by Marvin Meyers. Indianapolis: Bobbs-Merrill, 1973.

Montesquieu, Charles de Secondat, baron de. *The Spirit of the Laws*. Translated by Thomas Nugent. New York: Hafner, 1949. Bks. 6, 11, 12, 19, 26.

Nozick, Robert. *Anarchy, State, and Utopia*. New York: Basic Books, 1974.

Paine, Thomas. *The Rights of Man*. New York: Penguin, 1984.

Pease, William, and Jane Pease. *The Antislavery Argument*. Indianapolis: Bobbs-Merrill, 1965.

Pernock, Roland, and John Chapman, eds. *Human Rights*. New York: New York University Press, 1981.

Plato, *Republic*. Translated by Allan Bloom. New York: Basic Books, 1968. Bk. 5.

Rae, Douglas, et al. *Equalities*. Cambridge: Harvard University Press, 1981. Chap. 4.

Rawls, John. *A Theory of Justice*. Cambridge: Belknap Press of Harvard University Press, 1971.

Rossiter, Clinton, ed. *The Federalist Papers*. New York: New American Library, 1961.

Rousseau, Jean-Jacques. *Emile*. Translated by Allan Bloom. New York: Basic Books, 1979. Bks. 4, 5.

—— *Politics and the Arts: Letter to M. d'Alembert on the Theatre*. Translated by Allan Bloom. Ithaca: Cornell University Press, 1968.

—— *Social Contract*. Translated by Maurice Cranston. New York: Penguin, 1968.

Ryan, William. *Equality*. New York: Pantheon, 1981.

Sandel, Michael. *Liberalism and the Limits of Justice*. Cambridge: Cambridge University Press, 1982.

Strauss, Leo. *Natural Right and History*. Chicago: University of Chicago Press, 1953. Chap. 5.

Tawney, Richard. *Equality*. New York: Capricorn, 1961.

Tocqueville, Alexis Charles de. *Democracy in America*. Translated by Henry Reeve, revised by Francis Bowen. New York: Vintage Books, 1961. Vol. 2, pt. 3, chaps. 8–12.

Walzer, Michael. *Spheres of Justice: A Defense of Pluralism and Equality*. New York: Basic Books, 1983.

Young, Michael. *The Rise of Meritocracy*. Harmondsworth: Penguin, 1961.

ARTICLES

Cohen, G. A. "Freedom, Justice, and Capitalism." *New Left Review*, no. 126 (March–April 1981), pp. 3–16.

Daniels, Norman. "Merit and Meritocracy." *Philosophy and Public Affairs* 7 (Spring 1978): 206–23.

Dworkin, Ronald. "Liberalism." In *Public and Private Morality*, edited by Stuart Hampshire. Cambridge: Cambridge University Press, 1978.

Galston, William. "Defending Liberalism." *American Political Science Review* 76 (September 1982): 621–29.

Gibbard, Allan. "Natural Property Rights." *Nous* 10 (March 1976): 77–86.

Ryan, Cheney C. "Yours, Mine, and Ours: Property Rights and Individual Liberty." In *Reading Nozick*, edited by Jeffrey Paul. Totowa, N.J.: Rowman & Littlefield, 1981.

Scanlon, Thomas. "Nozick on Rights, Liberty, and Property." In *Reading Nozick*, edited by Jeffrey Paul. Totowa, N.J.: Rowman & Littlefield, 1981.

Schaar, John. "Equality of Opportunity, and Beyond." In *Equality*, edited by Roland Pennock and John Chapman. New York: Atherton, 1967.

Social Philosophy and Policy. Vol. 1, *Distributive Justice*. Oxford: Blackwell, 1983.

Stanley, John. "Equality and Opportunity as Philosophy and Ideology." *Political Theory* 5 (February 1977): 61–94.

Varian, Hal. "Distributive Justice, Welfare Economics, and the Theory of Fairness." *Philosophy and Public Affairs* 4 (Spring 1975): 223–47.

Williams, Bernard. "The Idea of Equality." In *Philosophy, Politics, and Society*, edited by Peter Laslett and W. G. Runciman. 2d ser. Oxford: Basil Blackwell, 1962.

Notes on the Contributors

WALTER BERNS is John M. Olin Distinguished Scholar in Constitutional and Legal Studies at the American Enterprise Institute and Professorial Lecturer at Georgetown University. Among the organizations of which he is a member are the National Council on the Humanities and the Council of Scholars in the Library of Congress. His books include *Freedom, Virtue, and the First Amendment*; *The First Amendment and the Future of American Democracy*; *For Capital Punishment: Crime and Morality of the Death Penalty*; and *In Defense of Liberal Democracy*.

ALLAN BLOOM is a professor in the Committee on Social Thought and the College at the University of Chicago and is co-director of the John M. Olin Center for Inquiry into the Theory and Practice of Democracy there. He is co-author of *Shakespeare's Politics* and has translated and supplied commentaries on Plato's *Republic* and Rousseau's *Emile*. His most recent book, *The Soul without Longing*, will appear soon. He is a member of the editorial board of *Political Theory* and *Commentaire*.

G. A. COHEN is Chichele Professor of Social and Political Theory and Fellow of All Souls, Oxford. He is author of *Karl Marx's Theory of History: A Defence* and of numerous articles on Marxism and social philosophy. His current interest is in the problems of freedom and justice in capitalist and socialist societies.

WILLIAM GALSTON is currently Director of Economic and Social Programs at the Roosevelt Center for American Policy Studies. His publications include *Kant and the Problem of History; Justice and the Human Good*; and articles in ethics and political philosophy, including "Defending Liberalism."

JUDITH N. SHKLAR is John Cowles Professor of Government at Harvard University. Among her books are *After Utopia*; *Legalism, Men, and Citizens*; *Freedom and Independence*; and *Ordinary Vices*. She is on the editorial board of *Daedalus* and *Political Theory*.

CHARLES TAYLOR is Professor of Political Science at McGill University. He was formerly Chichele Professor of Social and Political Theory at the University of Oxford, 1976–1981, and a member of the Institute for Advanced Study, Princeton, 1981–1982. His publications include *The Explanation of Behaviour*; *Hegel*; *Hegel and Modern Society*; and two volumes of *Philosophical Papers*.

MICHAEL WALZER is Professor of Social Science at the Institute for Advanced Study at Princeton. Among his books are *The Revolution of the Saints: A Study in the Origins of Radical Politics*; *Obligations: Essays on Disobedience*; *War and Citizenship*; *Just and Unjust Wars*; and, most recently, *Spheres of Justice: A Defense of Pluralism and Equality*. He is the editor of *Dissent*, a member of the editorial board of *Philosophy and Public Affairs*, and contributing editor of *The New Republic*.

Index

INDEX

Library of Congress Cataloging-in-Publication Data

Main entry under title:

Justice and equality here and now.

   Bibliography: p.
   Includes index.
   1. Distributive justice—Addresses, essays, lectures. 2. Justice—Ad-
dresses, essays, lectures. 3. Equality—Addresses, essays, lectures.
I. Lucash, Frank S., 1938–   . II. Shklar, Judith N.
JC578.J874   1986   320'.01'1   85–19465
ISBN 0–8014–1807–0
ISBN 0–8014–9350–1 (pbk.)